Introduction

The quilts you make deserve to have labels as special as the quilts. A label is a wonderful way to express a sentiment on a gift and to let future quilt lovers know the origins of your handwork.

Since you may have little time to spend on making an elaborate label, we have collected thirty foundation-piecing patterns for you to use and personalize. If you haven't done foundation piecing before, you are in for a treat. Follow our instructions on pages 2 to 8 and you'll soon be as enthusiastic about foundation piecing as we are.

You probably won't need any special supplies since most quilters already have what's needed—a pencil, permanent pen, fabric scraps left over from your quilt and your choice of foundation material. If you're feeling especially creative, you can add charms or other embellishments to make your label a true reflection of you.

General Directions

Supplies

The basic supplies you will need to complete a foundation-pieced label are:

- Foundation material (see below for options: paper, muslin or Tear Away®)
- Tracing materials (see Tracing the Label Pattern below)
- Assorted fabric scraps (including light-colored fabric for area to be written on)
- Sewing thread
- Permanent marking pens
- Fusible interfacing

Optional: freezer paper, embroidery floss, buttons, lace, charms, seed beads

The Foundation Piecing Method

Foundation Material

Before you start sewing, you will have to decide the type of foundation on which to piece your labels. There are several options. Paper is a popular choice because it is readily available; copier paper, tracing paper or newsprint work well. After sewing, the paper is removed.

Another alternative for foundation piecing is cotton fabric or muslin that is light-colored and lightweight for easy tracing. Just remember that the fabric will add another layer. Also, if you use a fabric foundation, you will be able to hand piece your labels if that is your desire.

A third option for foundation material is Tear Away® or Fun-dation™ translucent non-woven material. Like muslin, it is light enough to see through for tracing, but like paper, it can be easily removed after sewing.

Mirror Images

Most of the foundation-pieced quilt labels are not symmetrical; therefore, a mirror image of the label pattern will be produced when pieced, **Fig 1**. With each numbered pattern (pages 9 to 32), there is also a small diagram showing how the label will look once it has been pieced. Use that diagram when choosing fabrics.

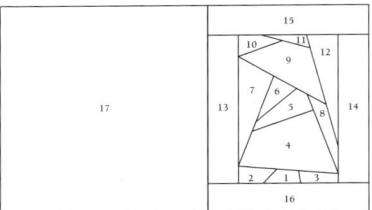

Foundation Pattern

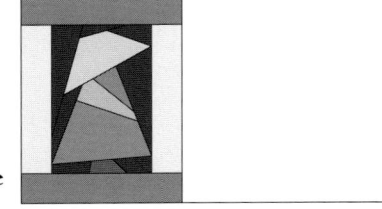

Fig 1 - Mirror Image

Preparing the Foundation

TRACING THE LABEL PATTERN

Trace the label pattern carefully onto your chosen foundation material. Use a ruler and a fine-point permanent marker or fine-line mechanical pencil to make straight lines; be sure to include all numbers. For ease in tracing, use a light box or tape pattern and fabric to a window.

TRANSFERRING THE LABEL

The label pattern can also be transferred onto foundation material by making your own iron-on transfer with a transfer pen or pencil. To do this involves an additional step if you want your label to look like the shaded diagram of the finished label. First, trace the label pattern onto tracing paper, **Fig 2**. Flop the paper so that the design is "backwards" and trace again onto plain paper using the transfer pen or pencil, **Fig 3**. Then, following manufacturers' directions, iron transferred design onto foundation material. If all these steps are not followed, your finished label will be a mirror image to the finished label shown, **Fig 4**.

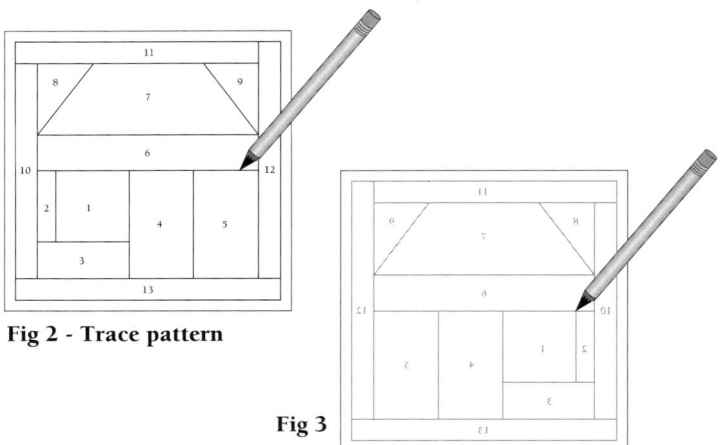

Fig 2 - Trace pattern

Fig 3

Flop and trace again

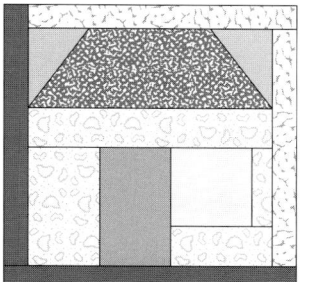
Fig 4 - Finished Label

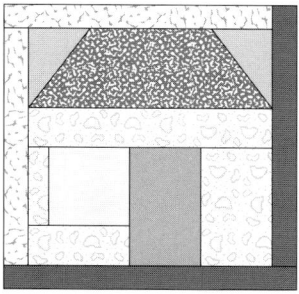
Mirror Image

Fabric

We recommend using 100% cotton fabric for piecing the quilt labels. By using cotton rather than cotton/polyester blends, the pieces will not slip as easily and they will respond better to finger pressing as you sew. For areas with messages, use a light-colored fabric on which the writing will show up. We recommend using solids, tone on tones or pastel prints. Also, be sure your fabric is light enough to see through if you are tracing your message.

Pre-washing fabric is not necessary, but you must test your fabric to make certain that the fabric is colorfast (don't trust manufacturers' labels). Place a 2"-wide strip (cut crosswise) of fabric into a bowl of extremely hot water; if the water changes color, the fabric is bleeding and it will be necessary to wash that fabric until all of the excess dye has washed out. Repeat for all fabrics that will be used. Fabrics that continue to bleed after they have been washed several times should be eliminated.

Cutting the Fabric

One of the biggest advantages to foundation piecing is that you do not have to cut every exact piece for every label. This is especially important for smaller labels or labels with many small pieces. It is much easier to handle a small strip of fabric than it is to handle a triangle where the finished size of the sides is 1/4".

The main consideration for using fabric pieces for a particular space is that the fabric must be at least 1/4" larger on all sides than the space it is to cover. Squares and strips are easy to figure, but triangle shapes can be a little tricky to piece. Use generous-sized fabric pieces and be careful when positioning the pieces onto the foundation. You do waste some fabric this way, but the time it saves in cutting will be worth it in the end.

Note: Before foundation-piecing your label, decide which method you will use to personalize it (see Personalizing Quilt Labels, page 6). If you will be printing information using a typewriter, copier or computer printer, you must do that prior to piecing your label.

How to Make a Foundation-Pieced Quilt Label

Prepare foundations as described in Preparing the Foundation, page 2.

Turn the foundation with unmarked side facing you and position piece 1 right side up over the space marked 1 on the foundation. Hold foundation up to a light source to make sure that the fabric overlaps at least 1/4" on all sides of space 1, **Fig 5**. Pin or use a glue stick to hold fabric in place.

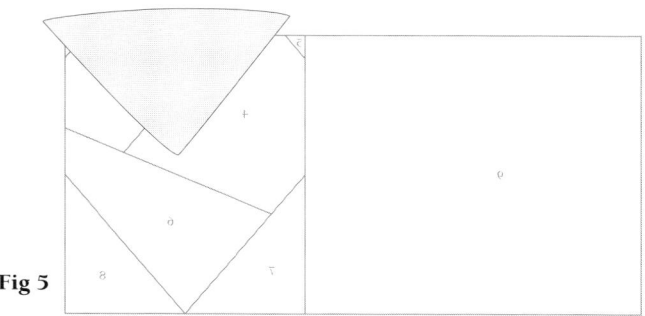
Fig 5

Hint: *Use only a small dab of a glue stick to hold fabric in place.*

Place fabric piece 2 right sides together with piece 1. Double check to see if fabric piece chosen will cover space 2 completely by folding over along line between space 1 and 2, **Fig 6**.

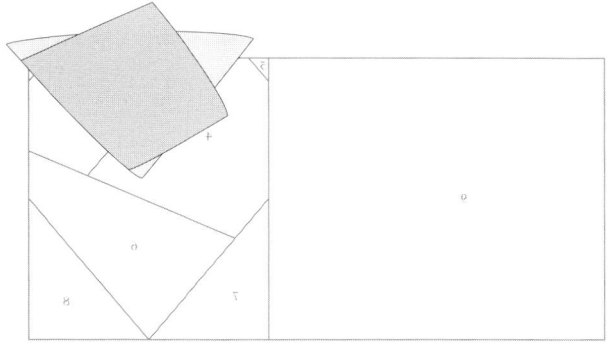

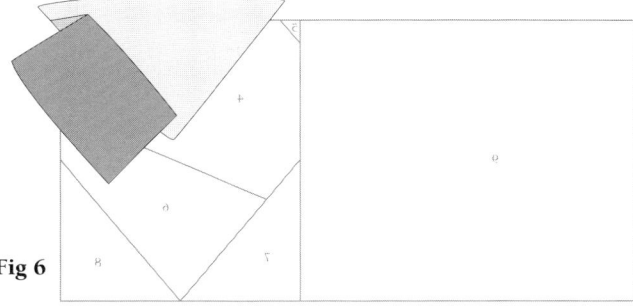
Fig 6

Turn foundation with marked side facing you and fold foundation forward along line between spaces 1 and 2; trim both pieces about 1/8" above fold, **Fig 7**. (You are actually pre-trimming the seam allowance of the first seam.)

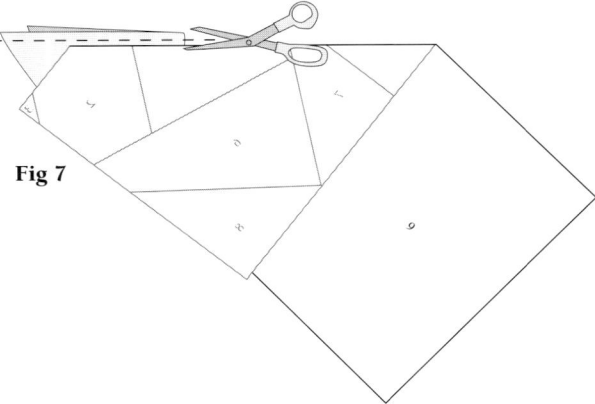

Fig 7

With marked side of foundation still facing you, place on sewing machine, holding fabric pieces in place. Sew along line between spaces 1 and 2 using a very small stitch (18 to 20 stitches per inch), **Fig 8**; begin and end sewing two to three stitches beyond line. You do not need to backstitch.

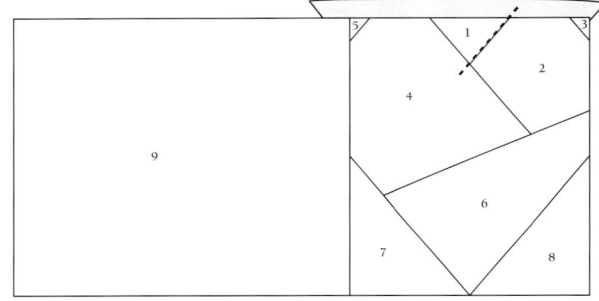

Fig 8

Hint: *Sewing with a very tiny stitch will allow for easier paper removal later. If paper falls apart after stitching, your stitch length is too small and you will need to lengthen the stitch slightly.*

Turn foundation over. Open piece 2 and finger press seam, **Fig 9**. Use a pin or dab of glue stick to hold piece in place if necessary.

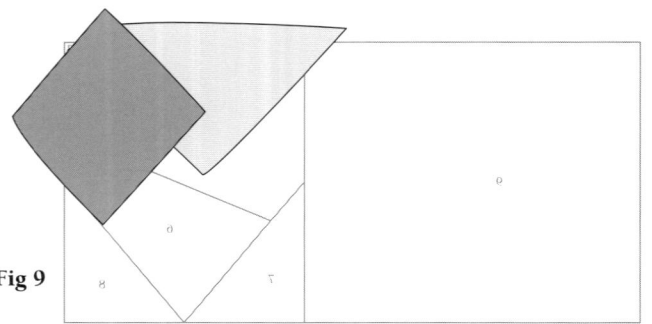

Fig 9

Turn foundation with marked side of foundation facing you; fold foundation forward along line between spaces 2 and 3 and trim about 1/8" from fold, **Fig 10**.

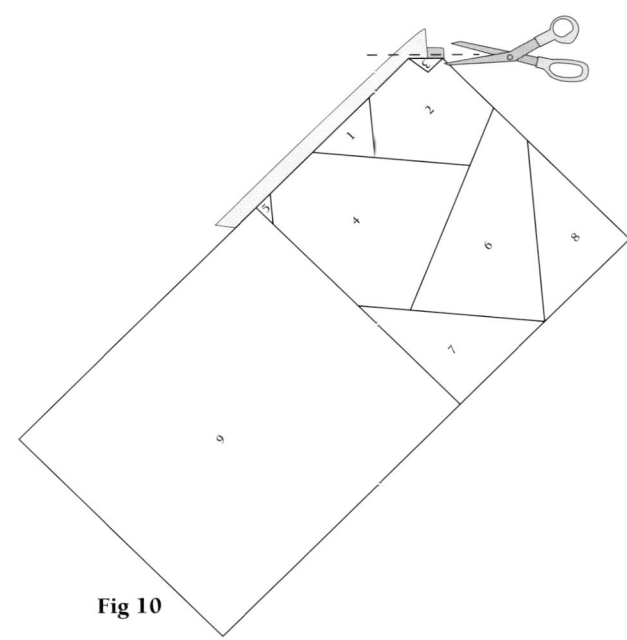

Fig 10

Hint: *If using a paper foundation, carefully pull paper away from stitching for easier trimming. If using a fabric foundation, fold it forward as far as it will go and trim.*

Place fabric piece 3 right side down even with just-trimmed edge, **Fig 11**.

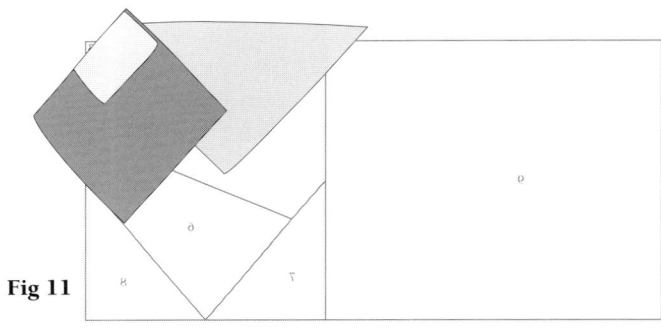

Fig 11

Turn foundation to marked side and sew along line between spaces 2 and 3; begin and end sewing two or three stitches beyond line, **Fig 12**.

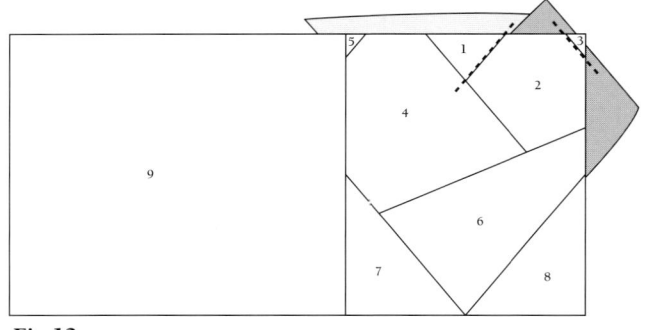

Fig 12

Turn foundation over, open piece 3 and finger press seam, **Fig 13**. Glue or pin in place.

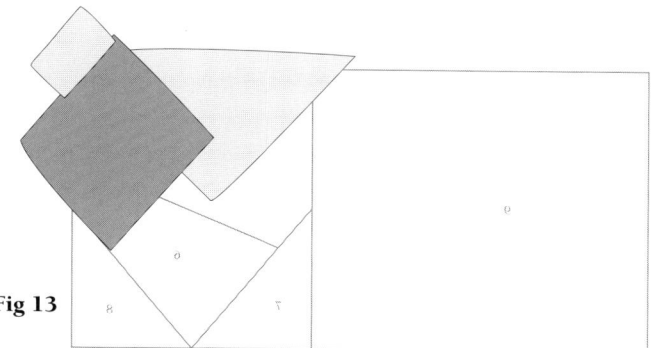
Fig 13

Turn foundation with marked side facing you. Fold foundation forward along line between spaces 1, 2, and 4; trim to about 1/8" from fold, **Fig 14**.

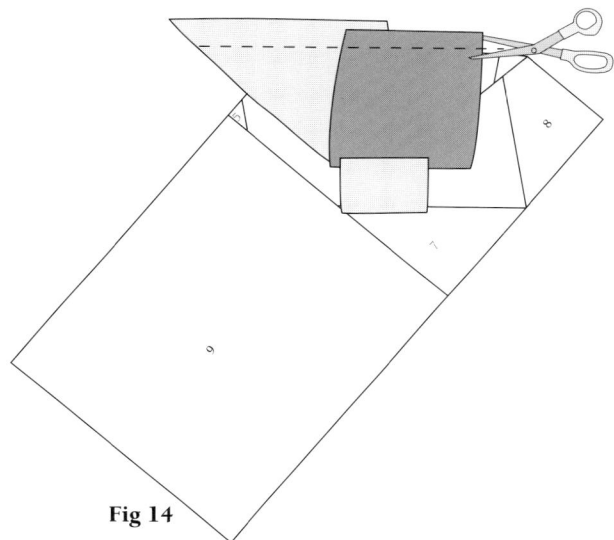
Fig 14

Place fabric piece 4 right side down even with just-trimmed edge. With marked side of foundation still facing you, sew along line between spaces 1, 2 and 4, **Fig 15**.

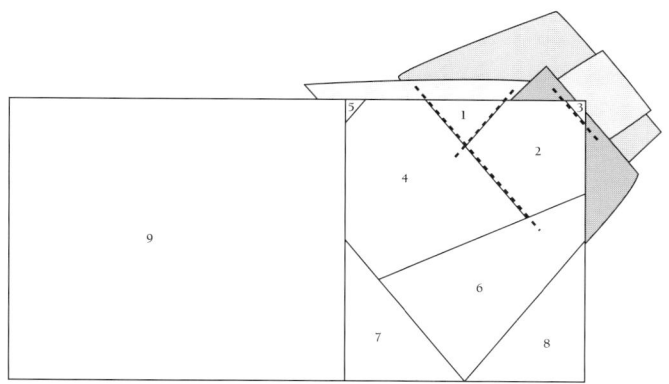
Fig 15

Continue trimming and sewing pieces in numerical order until label is complete, **Fig 16**. Make sure pieces along the outer edge are large enough to allow for the 1/4" seam allowance. Press label, then trim fabric 1/4" from outside line of foundation to complete label, **Fig 17**. Staystitch along edge of label, just outside outer line, **Fig 18**.

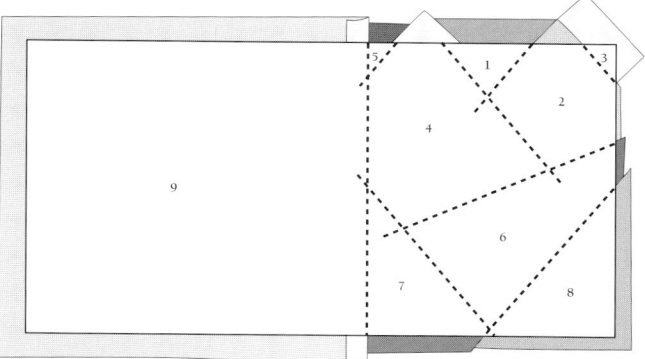
Fig 16

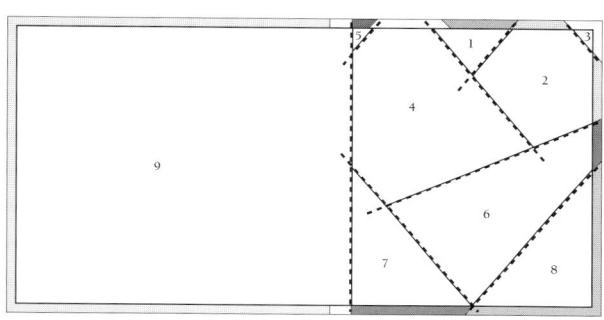
Fig 17

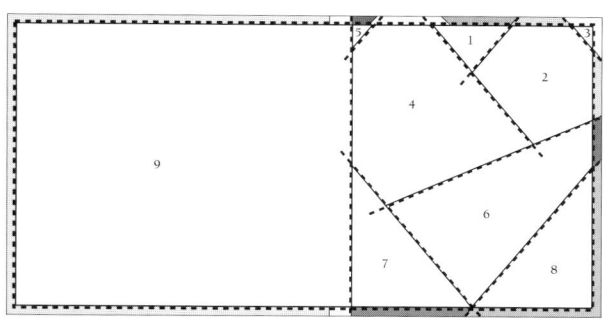
Fig 18

If using paper foundation, remove paper carefully.

Highlights and Hints for Foundation Piecing

- Begin and end sewing at least two to three stitches beyond line you are sewing on, **Fig 19**. Some of the labels have very tiny pieces, so don't worry if your stitching goes through a whole space and into another space, **Fig 20**; it will not interfere with adding subsequent pieces.

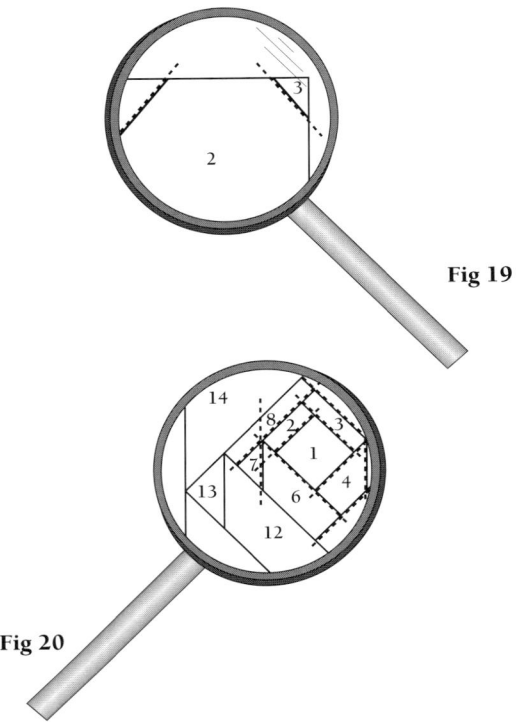

Fig 19

Fig 20

- Remember to use large enough pieces around outer edges to allow for a 1/4" seam allowance.
- Use a short stitch, around 20 stitches per inch.
- Trim seam allowances to 1/8" (or smaller if necessary).
- Finger press or press with an iron after every seam. The little wooden "irons" found in quilt shops or catalogs work great.
- When sewing spaces with points, it is easier to start sewing from the wide end towards the point, **Fig 21**.

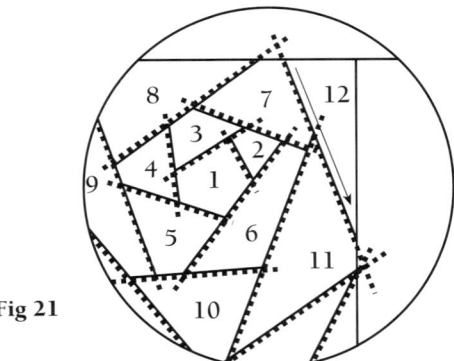

Fig 21

- Don't worry too much about grainline. Sewing to a foundation stabilizes the fabric and will prevent it from getting out of shape. Staystitching before removing paper also stabilizes the block.
- Directional prints are not recommended unless they are used only once in a label or placed where they can be used easily in a consistent manner, **Fig 22**.

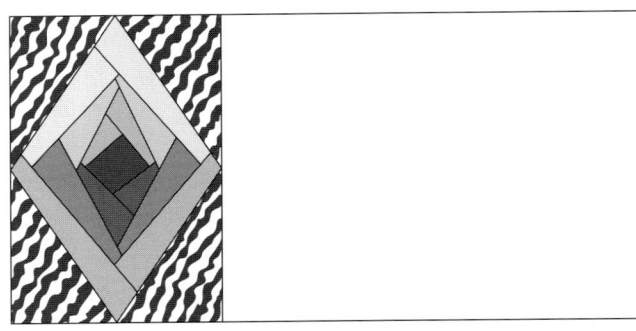

Like this

Fig 22 - Not this

Personalizing Quilt Labels

Personalize your quilt label with the desired information such as name(s), dates, location, occasion or celebration. You can even add the quilt name, block name, fabric origin and method used to make the quilt.

Writing/Tracing

The easiest way to personalize your quilt label is to write directly on it using permanent fabric marking pens. There are many different brands on the market. Choose one that is most comfortable. Fine-line markers are best for writing. Some brands of pens may need to be heat set in order to make them washable; some need to dry for an extended period of time. Be sure to follow the manufacturer's suggestions.

If you are a little intimidated by writing on your completed label, write out what you would like to say on paper in a space the same size as the message area of your label. When you are satisfied, trace message onto label, using a light source such as a light box, glass table with light underneath or tape your label with copy underneath to a window. Tape label to paper, centering message, to keep label from slipping.

If you are unsure about your own handwriting and have access to a computer, type your information with a simple font, print out and then trace onto label.

If you would rather embroider the information, write or trace onto the label with a regular lead pencil or water-soluble pen. Use a simple Stem Stitch, **Fig 23**, or Backstitch, **Fig 24** to cover lines.

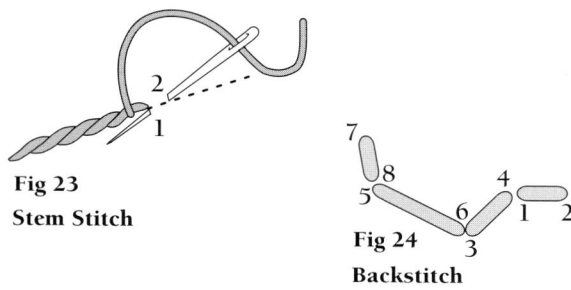

Fig 23
Stem Stitch

Fig 24
Backstitch

Other Methods

You can also personalize your quilt label using a typewriter, computer printer or copier. These require that you add information to the fabric before foundation piecing your label.

Trace message area onto paper side of an 8 1/2" x 11" piece of freezer paper using a permanent black marker. You should be able to see tracing from opposite side of paper.

Iron an 8 1/2" x 11" piece of fabric to shiny side of the 8 1/2" x 11" piece of freezer paper. Then do one of the following:

1. Place freezer paper/fabric in typewriter and begin typing on the fabric side inside the area marked on the freezer paper. Cut out 1/4" from drawn line.

2. Place freezer paper/fabric into paper tray of your computer printer and print information.

Note: Be sure to check which way to place fabric in tray. Look in your printer manual or check by placing a mark in the corner of a plain piece of paper in the paper tray. Print information and check to see if the marked side of the paper is on the side that printed. If it is, then place your fabric up in the paper tray; if not, place fabric face down.

3. If you have access to a copier, place freezer paper/fabric in paper tray, then copy information that you have typed or written out. ***Note:*** *First, be sure to check which way to place fabric in paper tray.*

Embellishing

Some of the labels can be embellished if desired.

"Border Crazy," page 10, was stitched along seams with Blanket Stitch (Fig 25) and Feather Stitch (Fig 26). Trim was added to remaining seams.

"Clever Kitty," page 12, has black and green seed beads for eyes, a black seed bead for nose and a pink seed bead for mouth. Whiskers were stem stitched (see **Fig 23**) with two strands of gray floss.

"With Love," page 14, was stitched along seams with the Blanket Stitch, **Fig 25** and Feather Stitch, **Fig 26**. Lace was sewn along one of the seams.

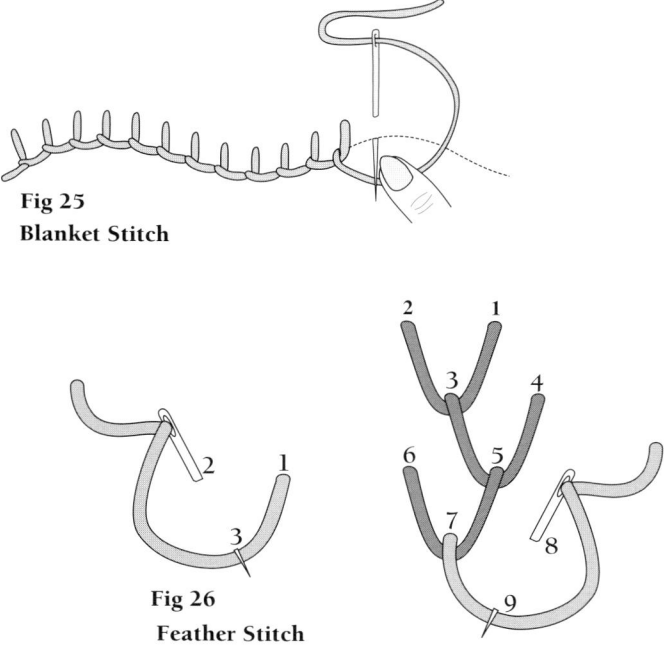

Fig 25
Blanket Stitch

Fig 26
Feather Stitch

"Victorian Fan," page 16, has lace sewn along the outside edge of the fan.

"Christmas Tree," page 18, has a star attached to top of tree.

"Button Basket," page 21, is filled with buttons and ribbon bows using 1/8"-wide ribbon.

"Puppy Dog," page 23, has black seed beads for eyes and nose and a red seed bead for mouth.

"Heavenly Angel's" eyes, page 27, were drawn with a brown fabric pen.

"Home Sweet Home," page 31, has a small button sewn on door.

Finishing Your Quilt Label

Once your label is sewn and personalized, it is ready to attach to your quilt back. We found that sewing a piece of fusible interfacing to back of quilt label works well to turn under edges (many of which contain several seam allowances due to foundation piecing).

1. Cut a piece of fusible interfacing the size of your label.

2. Place interfacing with bumpy (sticky) side together with right side of your quilt label.

3. Sew along all edges with a 1/4" seam allowance, **Fig 27**.

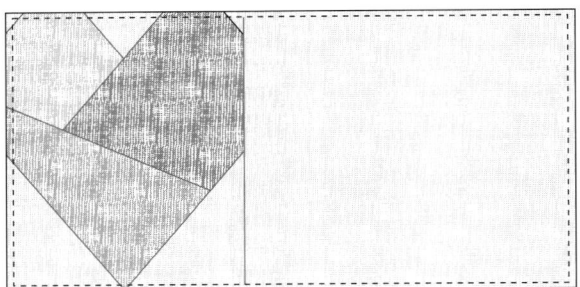

Fig 27

4. Carefully cut a 2" slit in the center of the interfacing, **Fig 28**. Turn label right side out through opening; bumpy side of interfacing will be facing out. Finger press along edges.

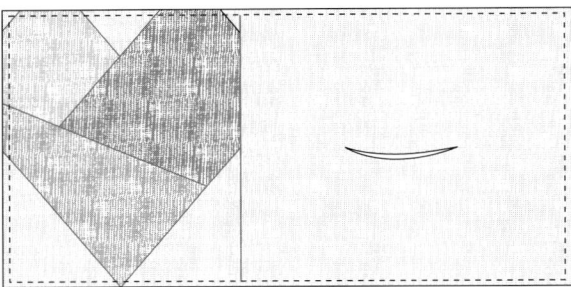

Fig 28

5. Iron label to back of quilt and Blindstitch in place, **Fig 29**.

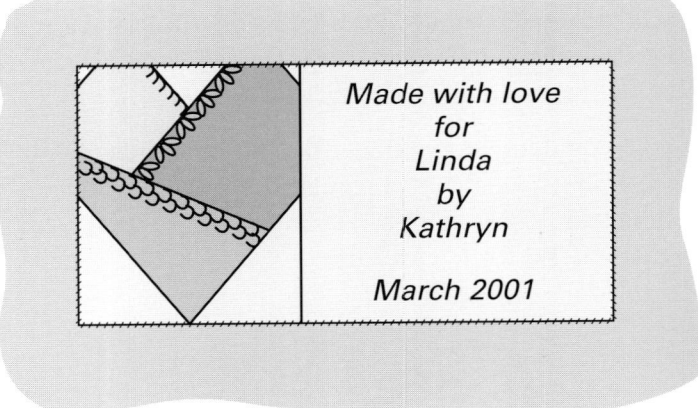

Fig 29

Optional: Use lightweight fabric or non-fusible interfacing and follow the steps above. Instead of ironing the label in place, just pin to quilt back and Blindstitch in place.

1 Berry Log Cabin

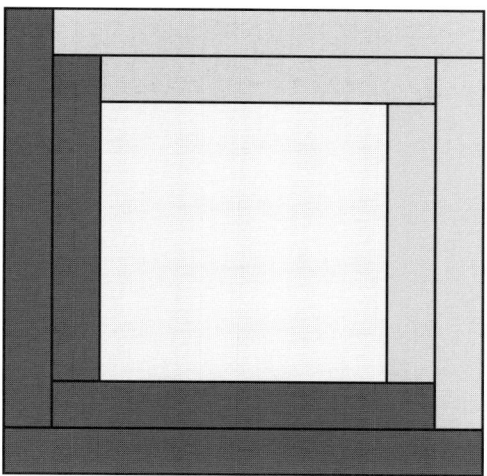

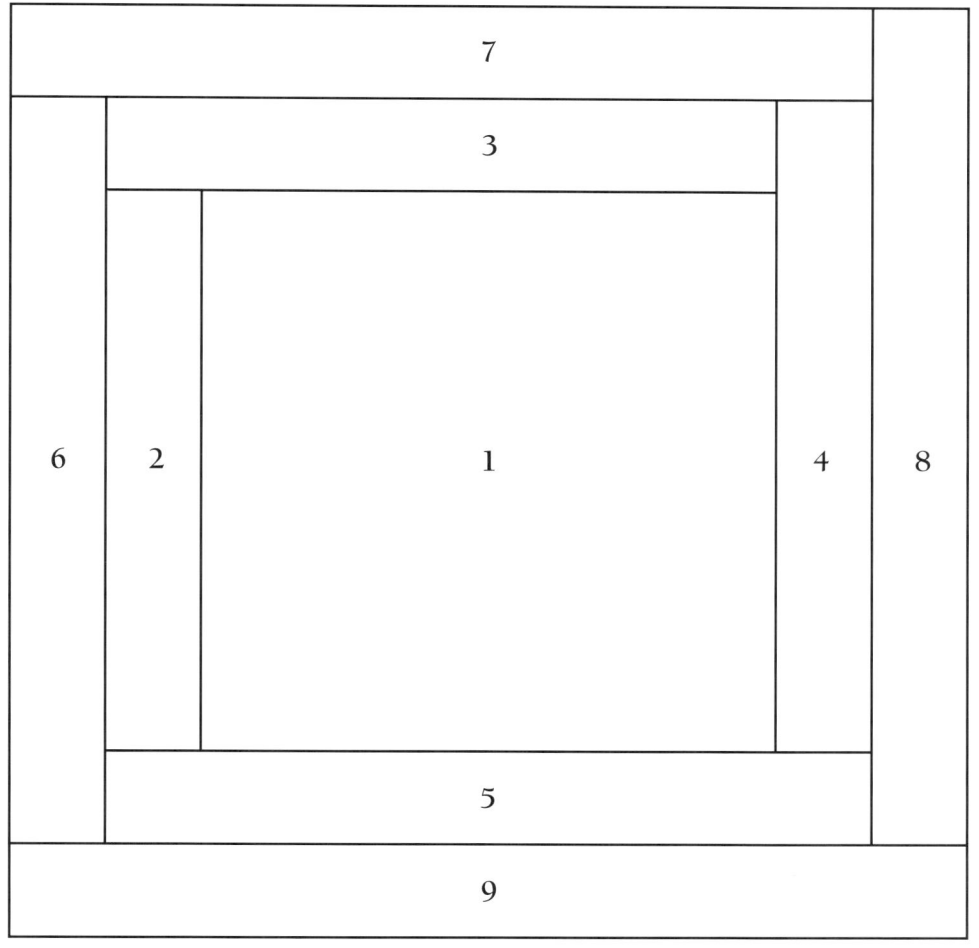

2 Border Crazy

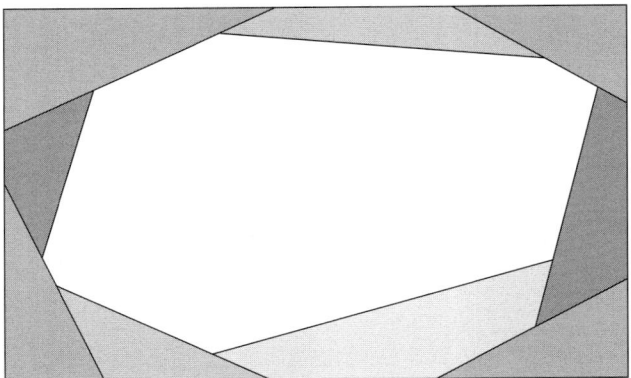

For embellishing, see page 7.

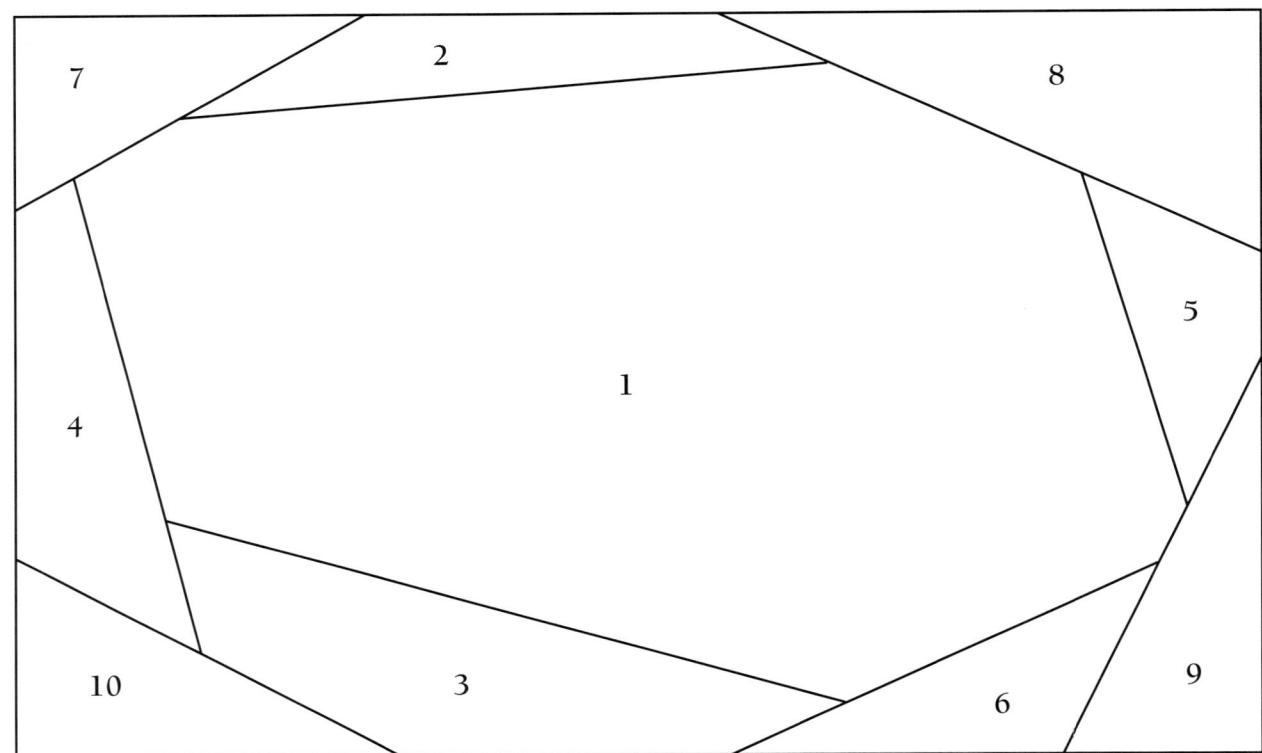

3 Octagon Rainbow

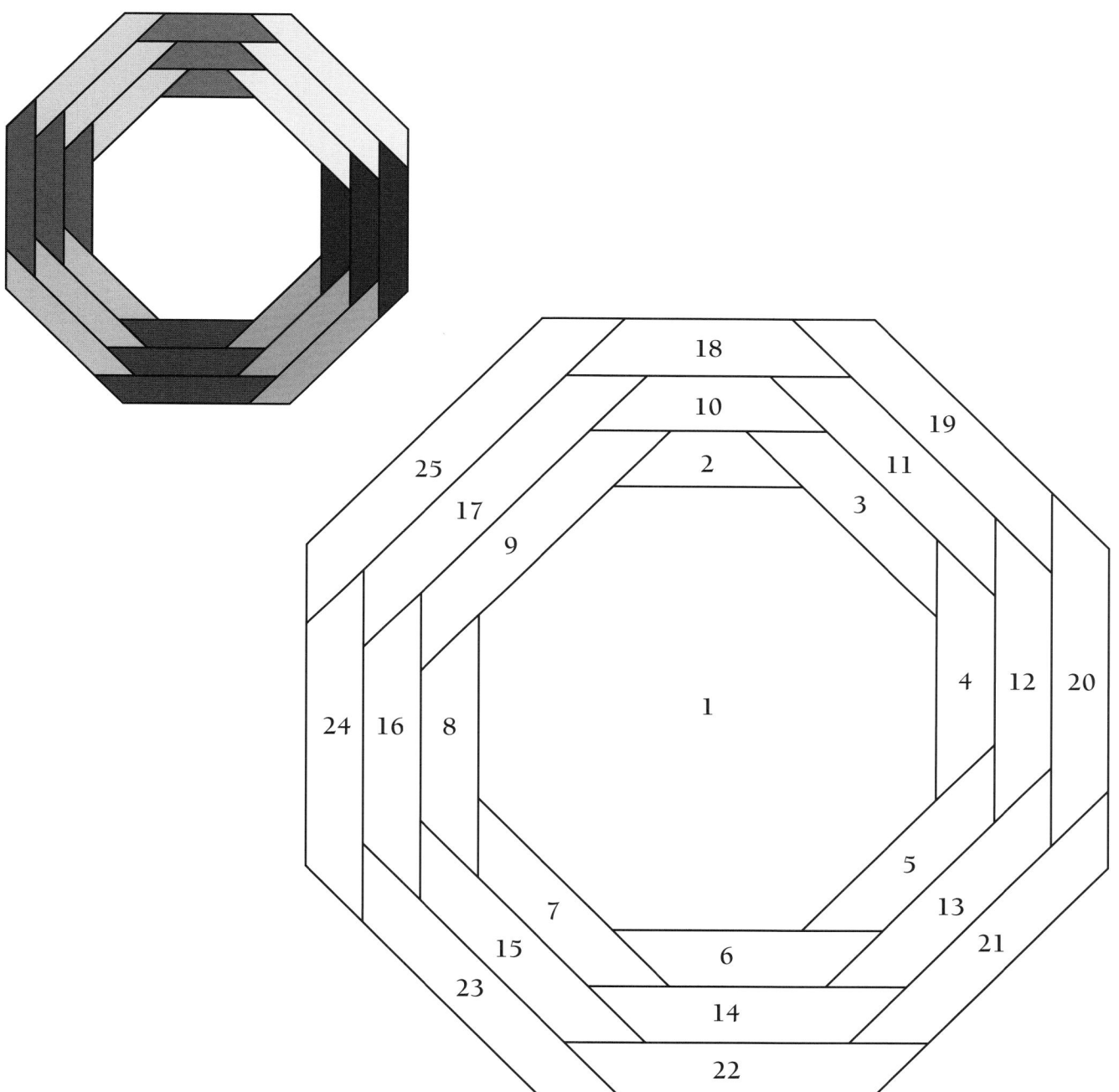

4 Crazy Rose

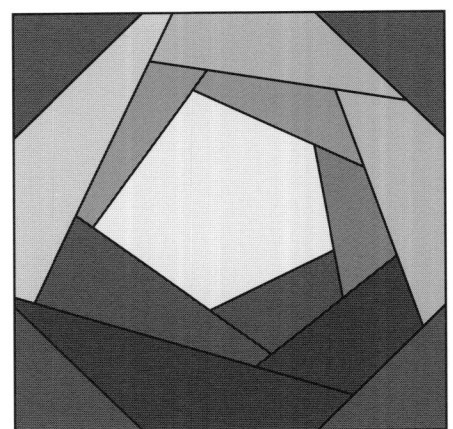
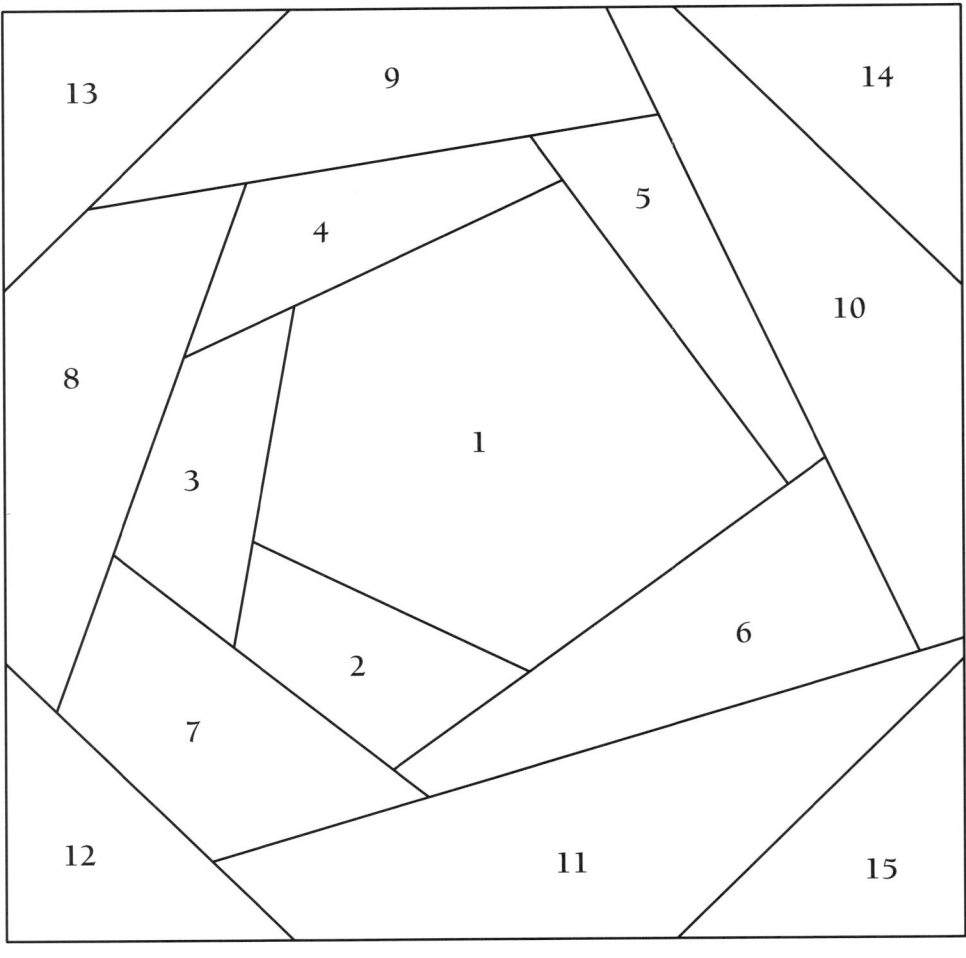

5 Clever Kitty

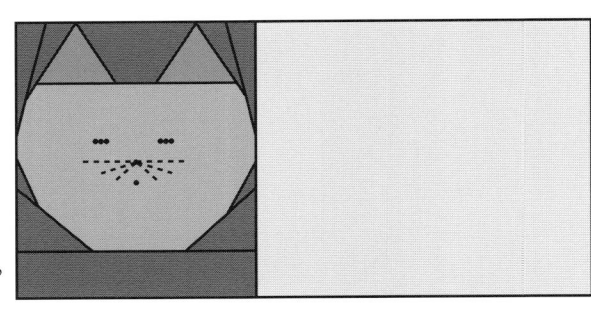

For embellishing, see page 7.

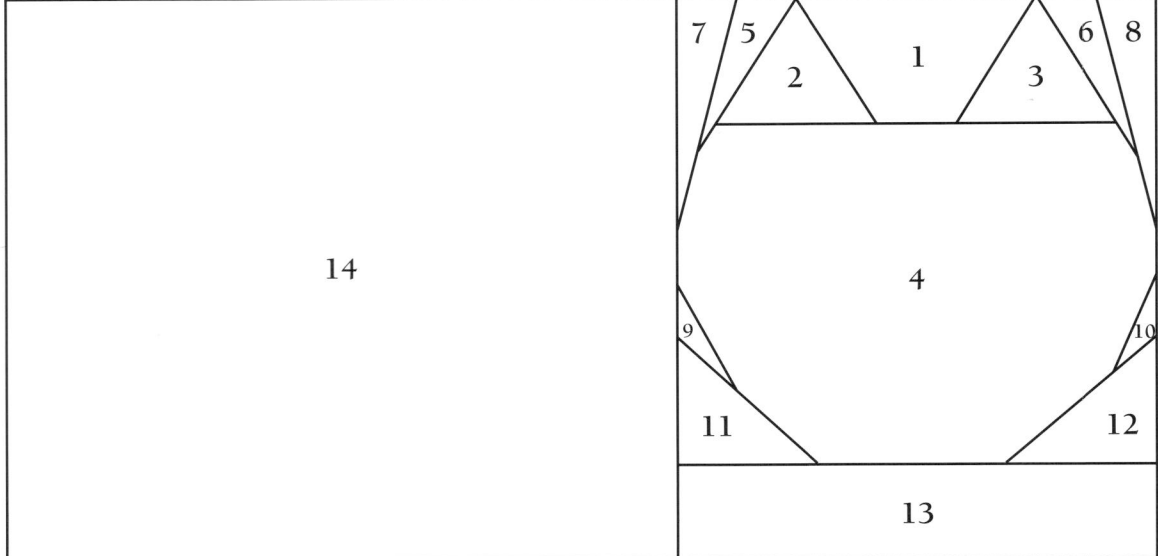

6 Framed Tulip

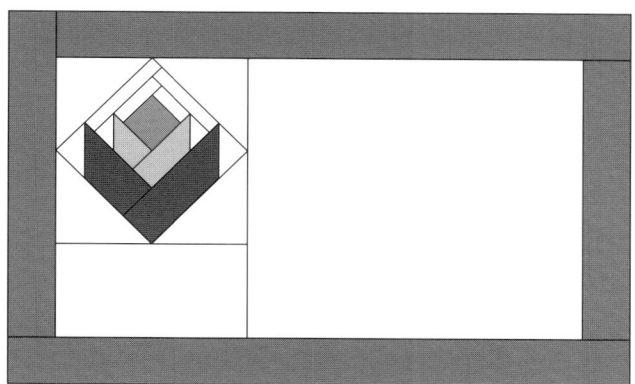

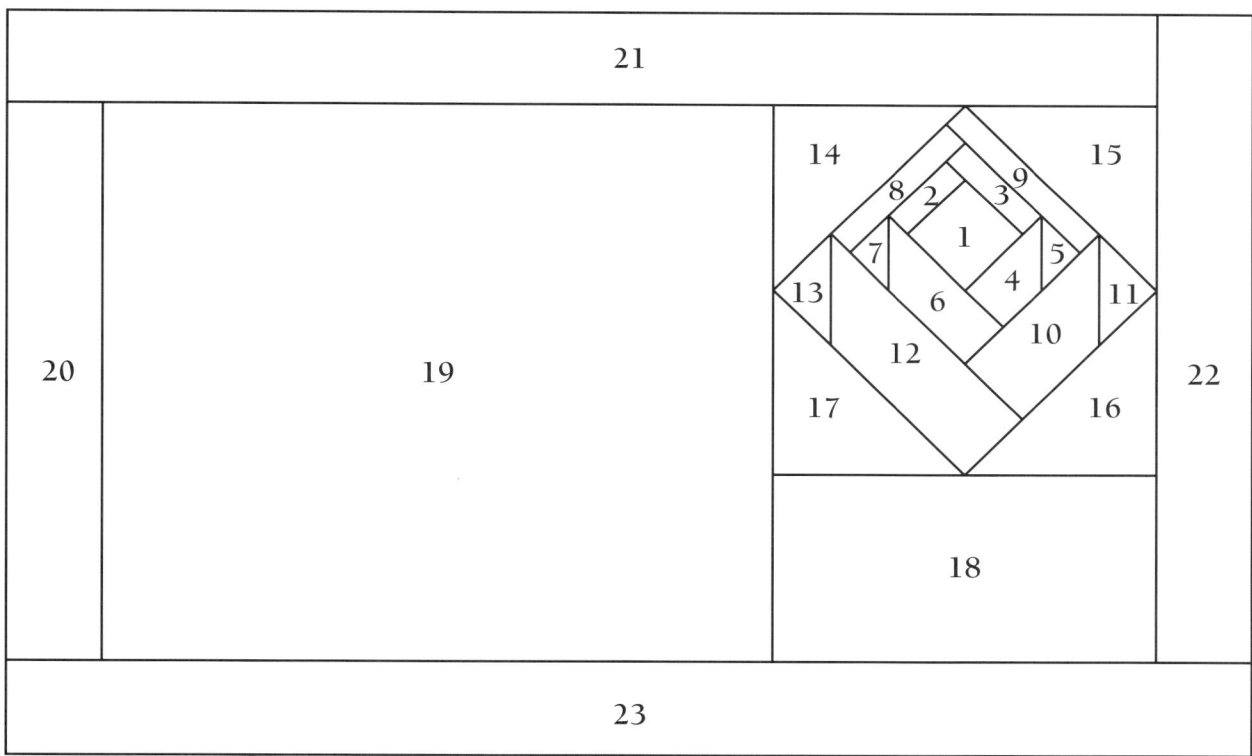

7 With Love

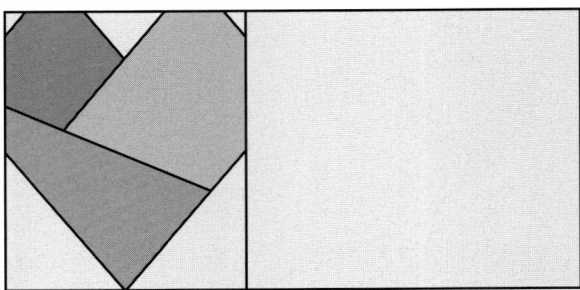

For embellishing, see page 7.

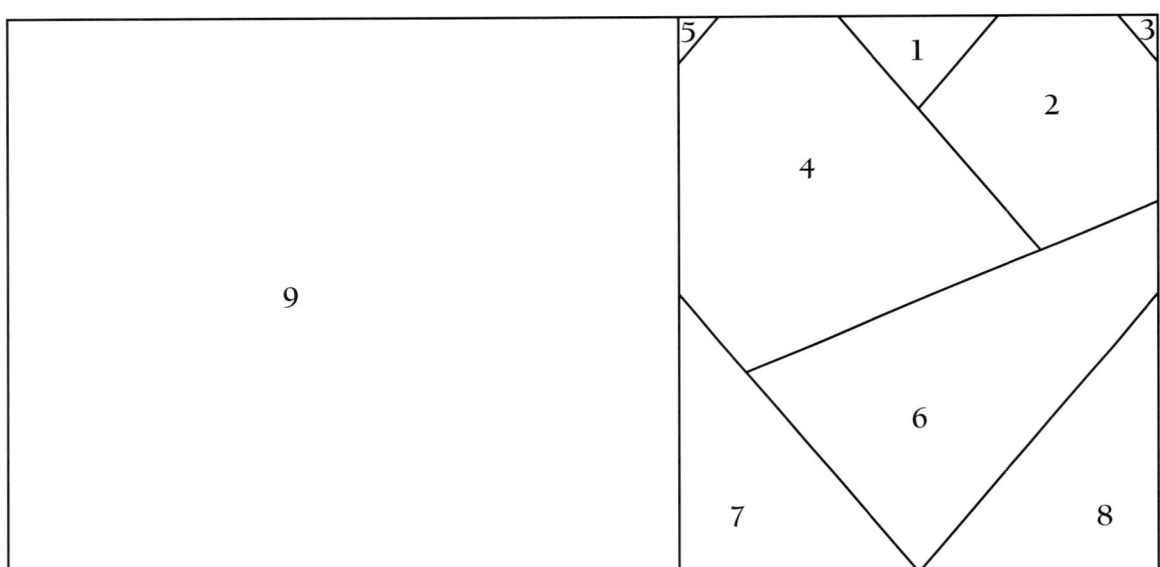

8 Sunbonnet Baby

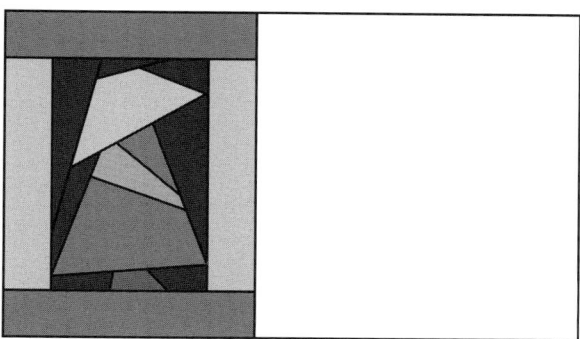

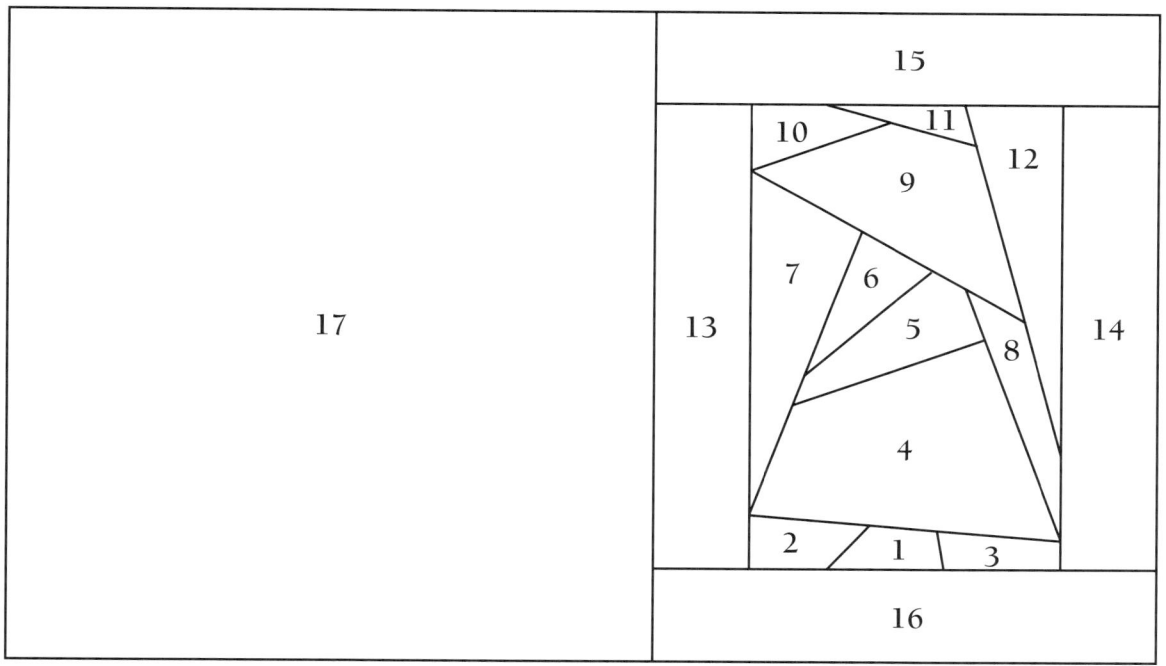

9 Victorian Fan

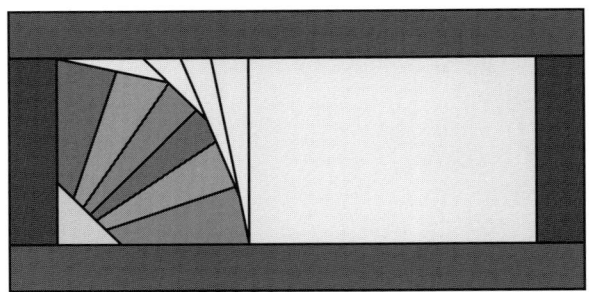

For embellishing, see page 7.

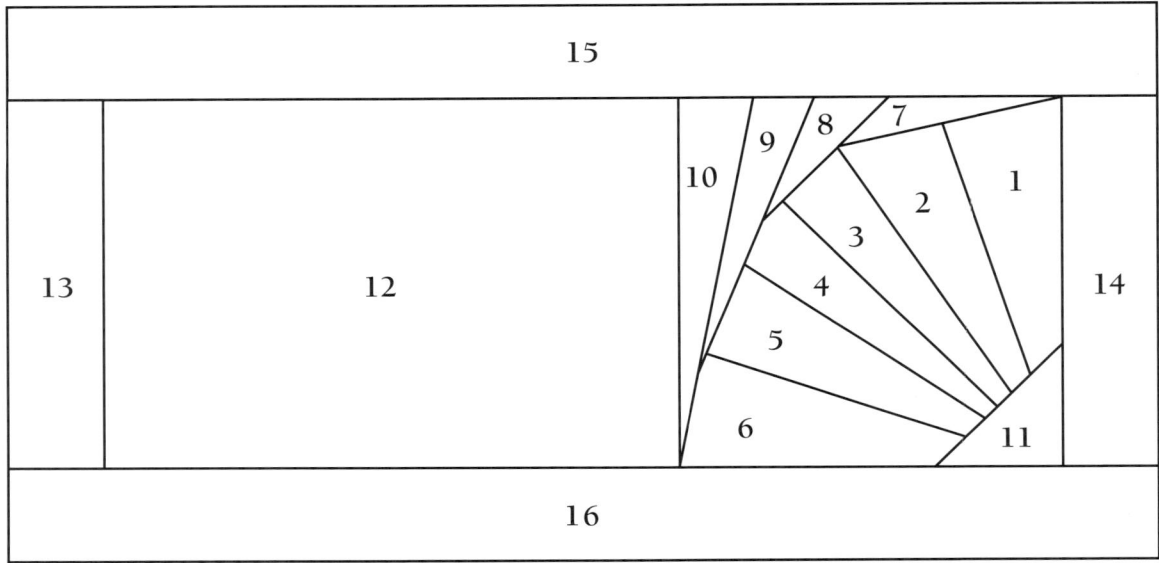

10 Square in a Square

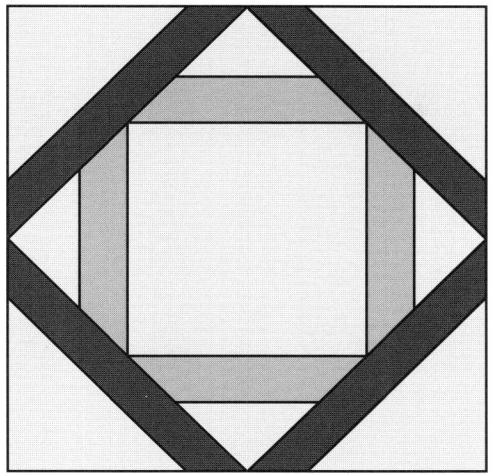

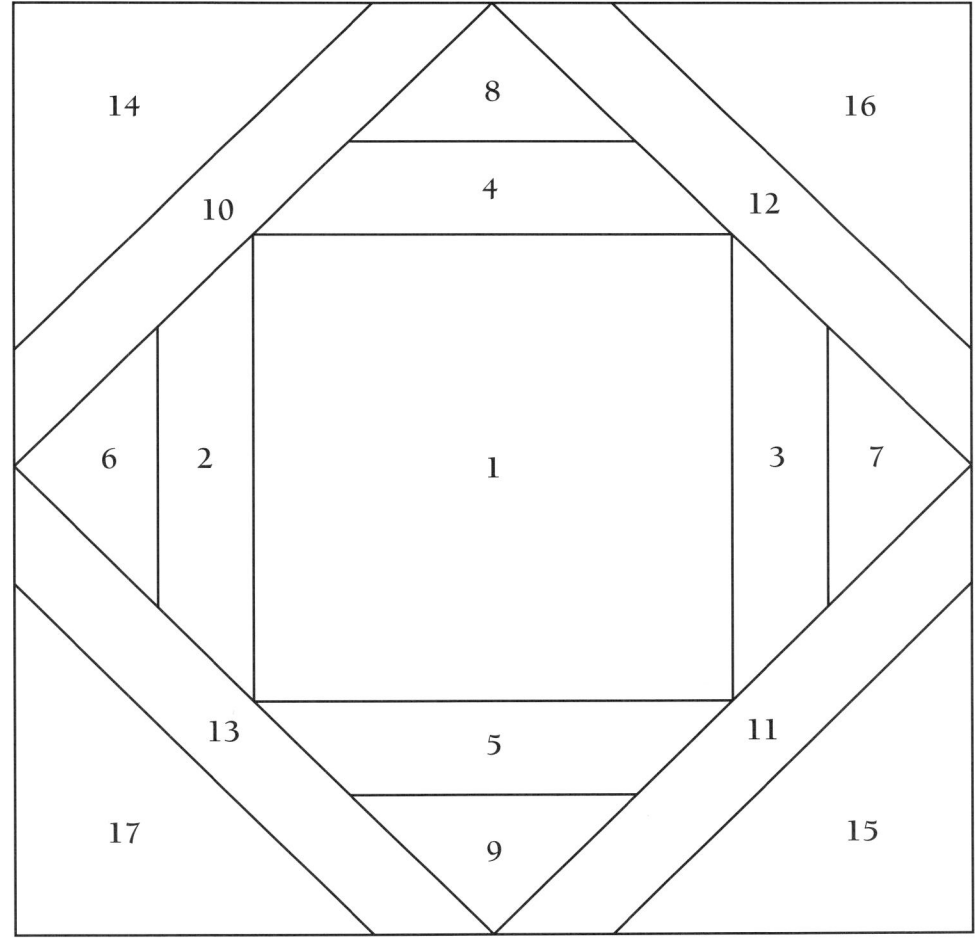

11 Christmas Tree

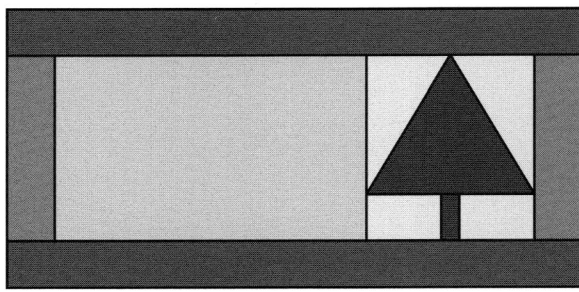

For embellishing, see page 7.

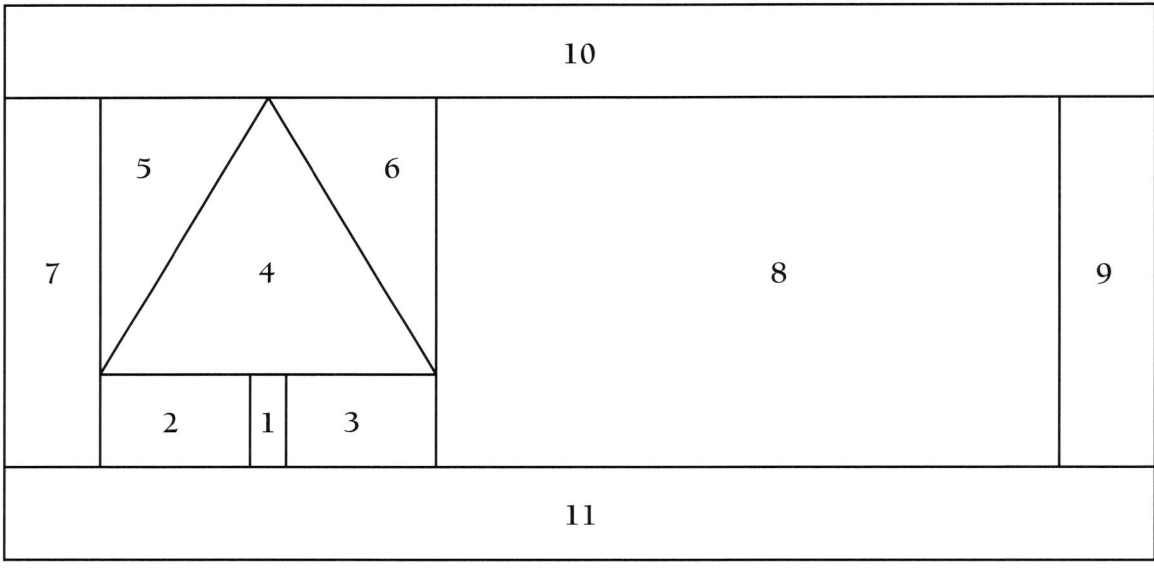

12 Flower Basket

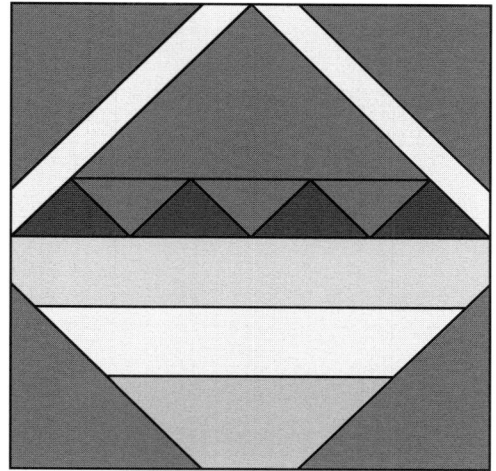

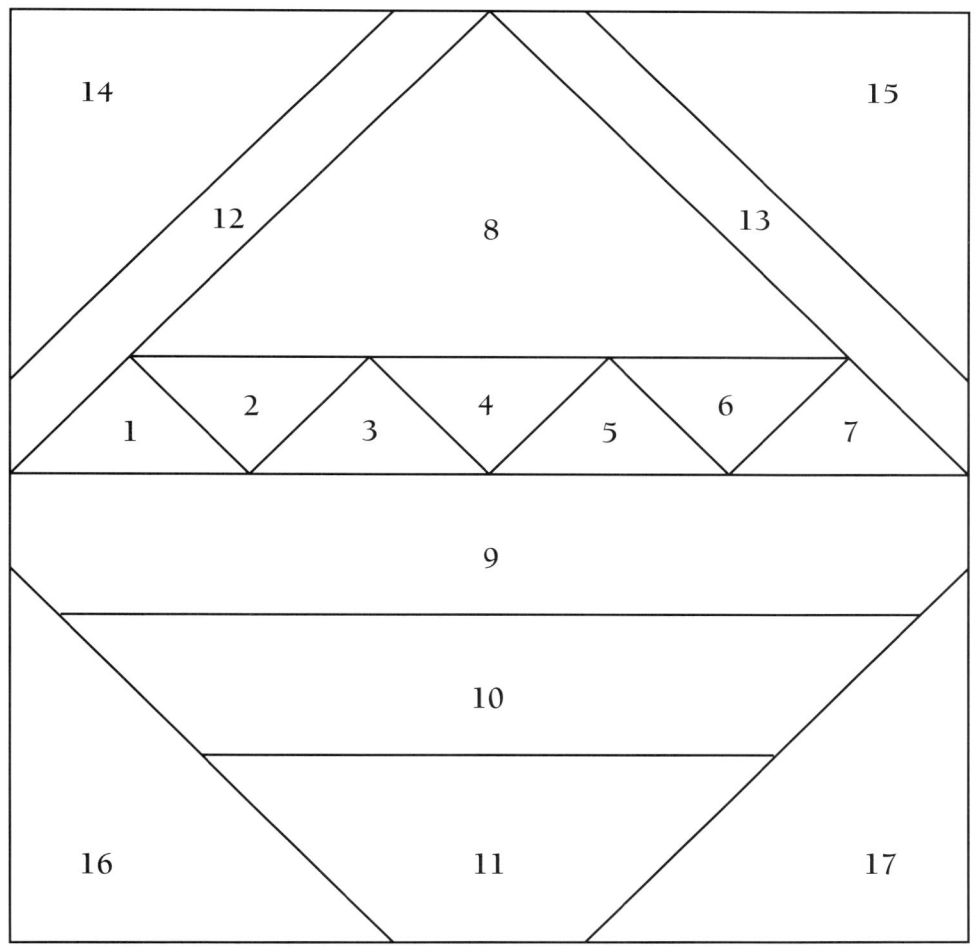

13 Diamond

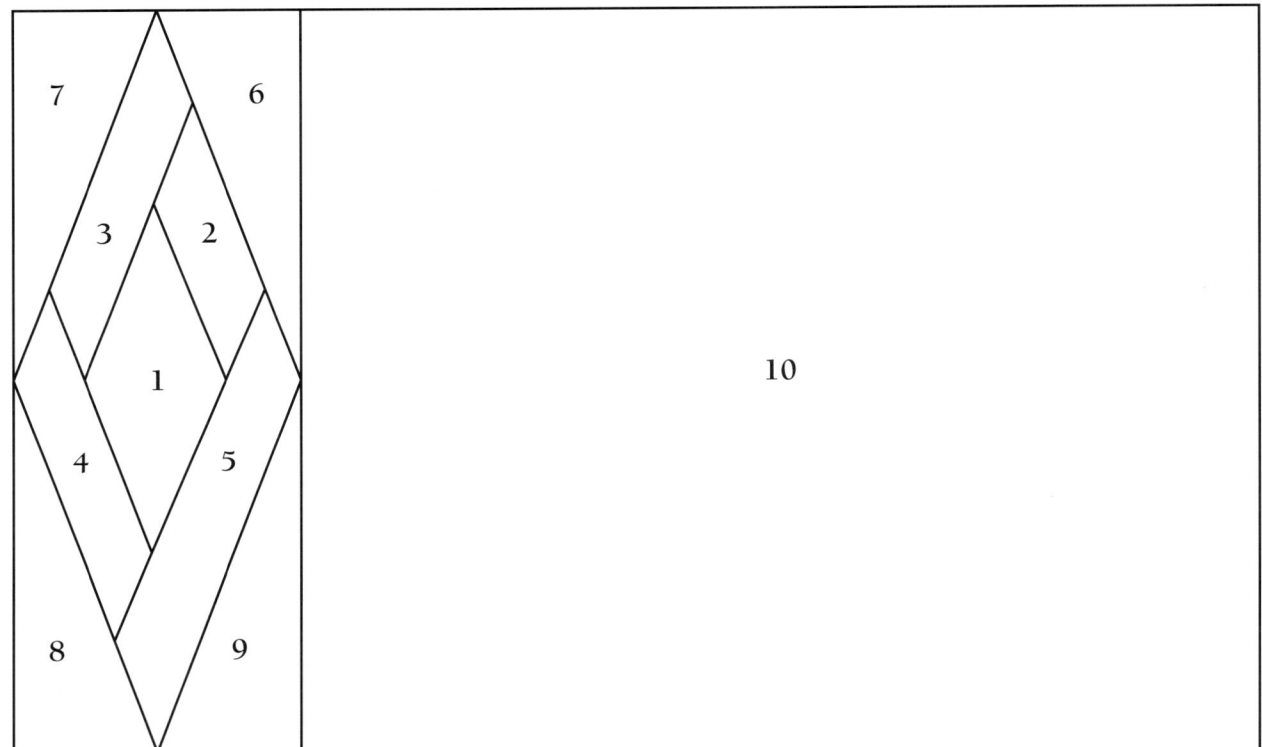

14 Button Basket

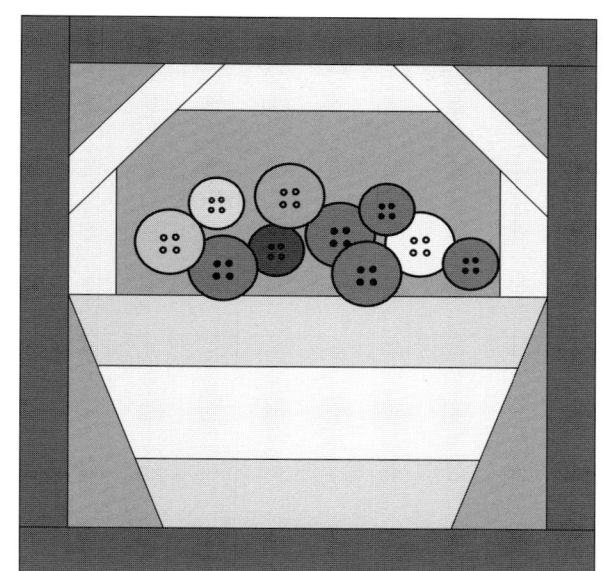

For embellishing, see page 7.

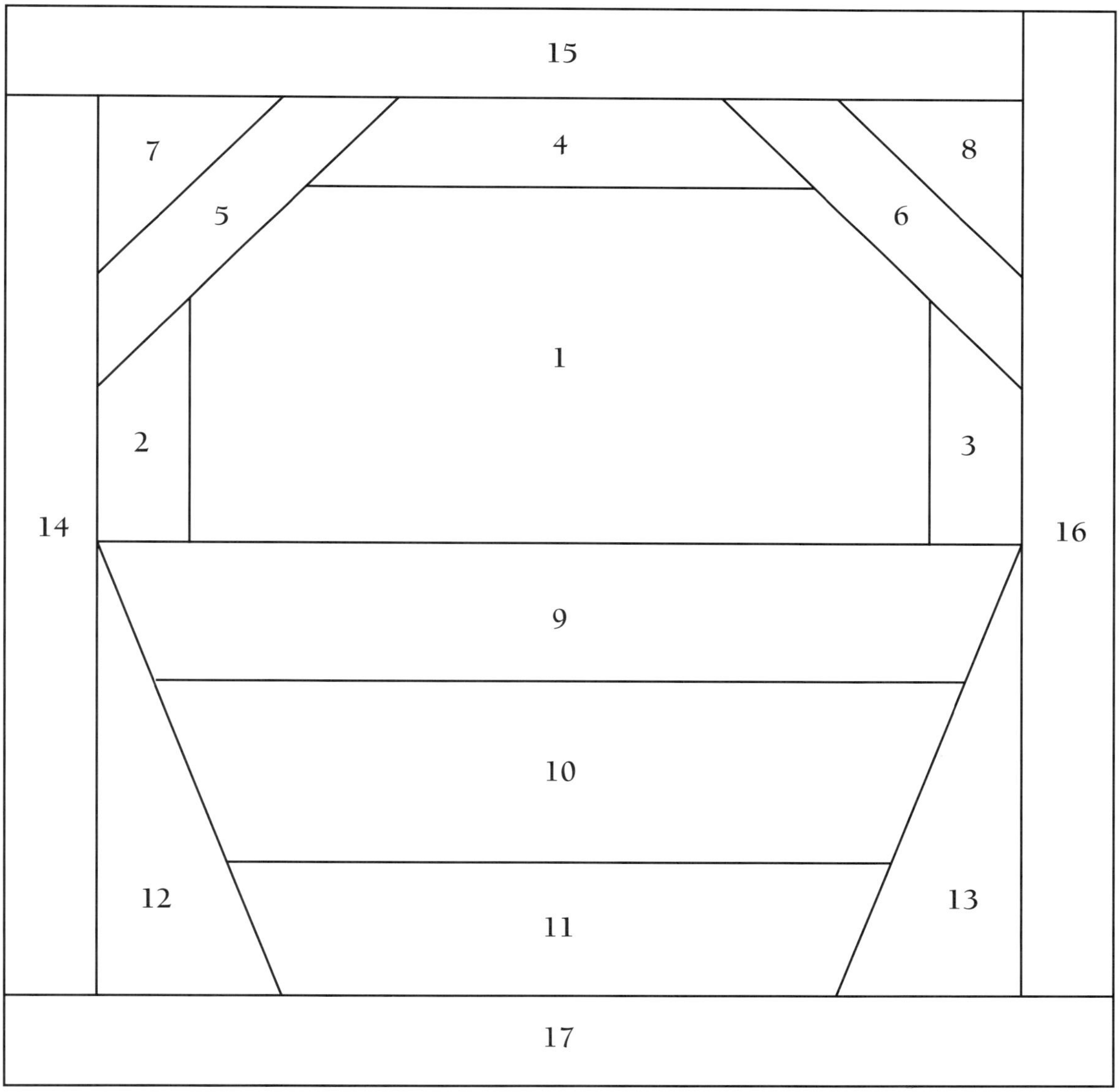

15 Log Cabin Flower

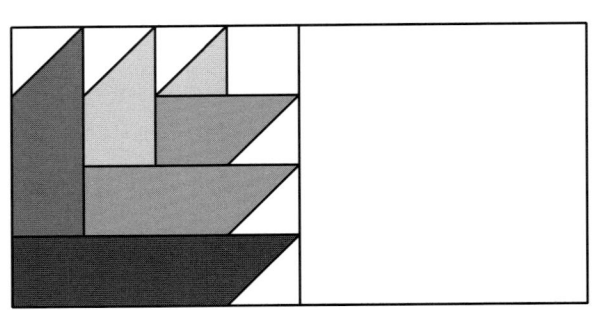

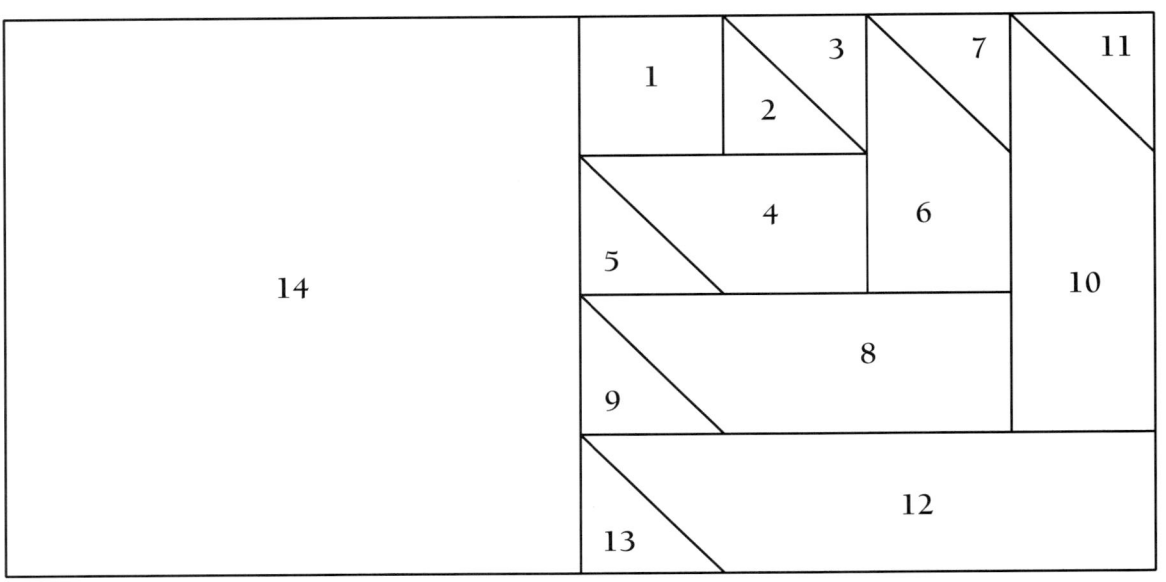

16 Crazy Bloom

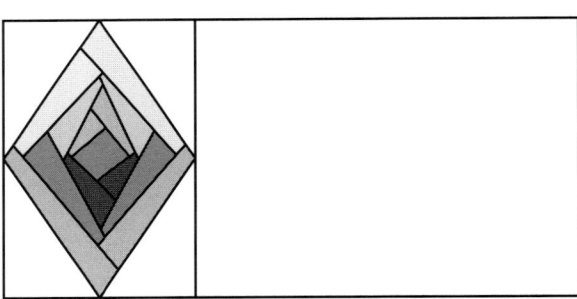

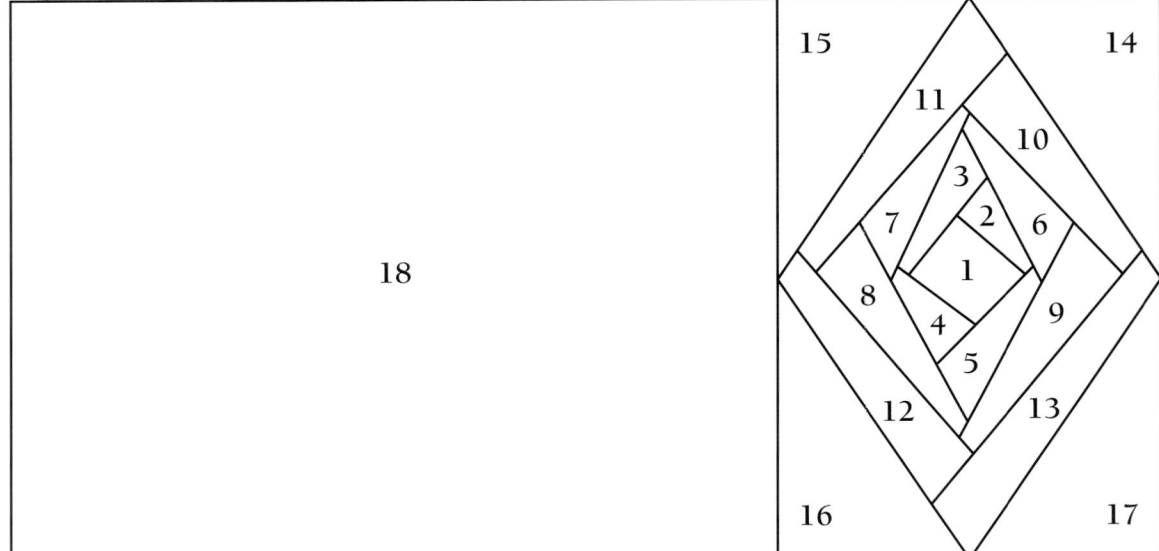

17 Puppy Dog

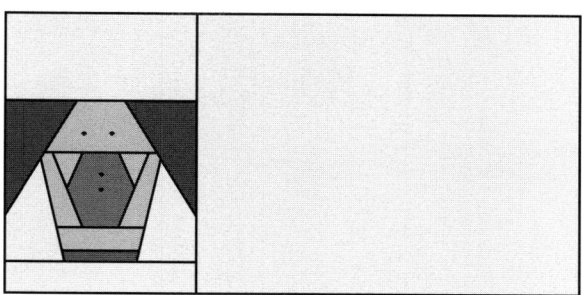

For embellishing, see page 7.

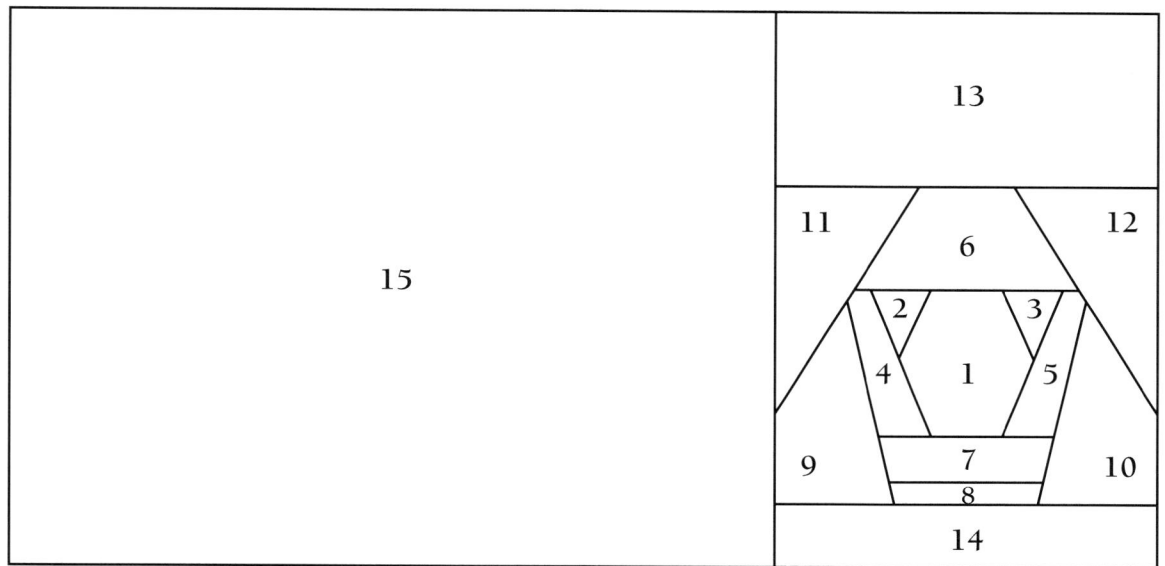

18 Love Triangles

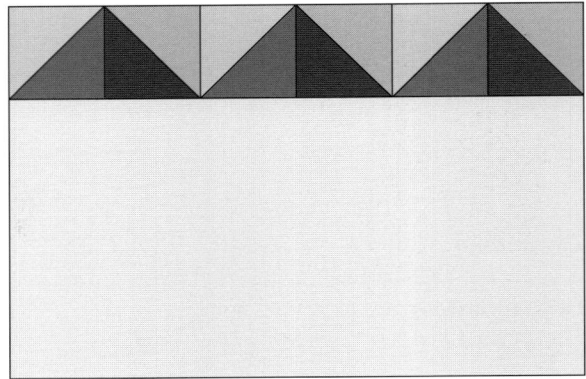

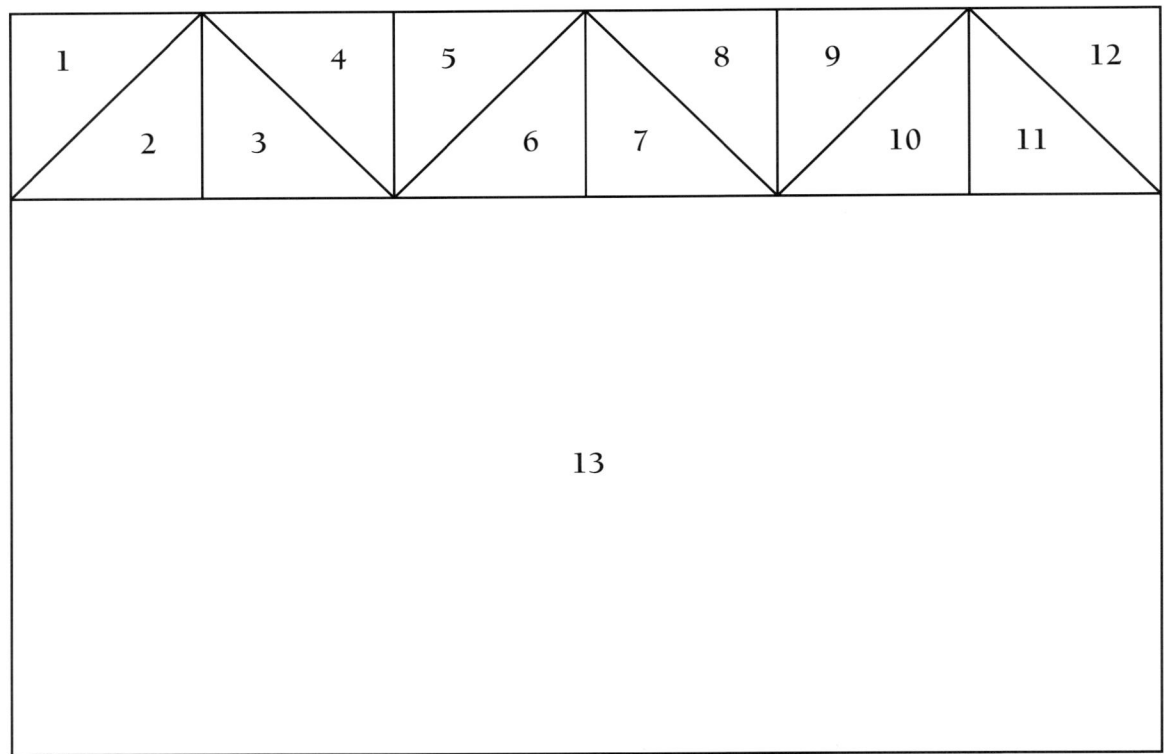

19
Flying Geese

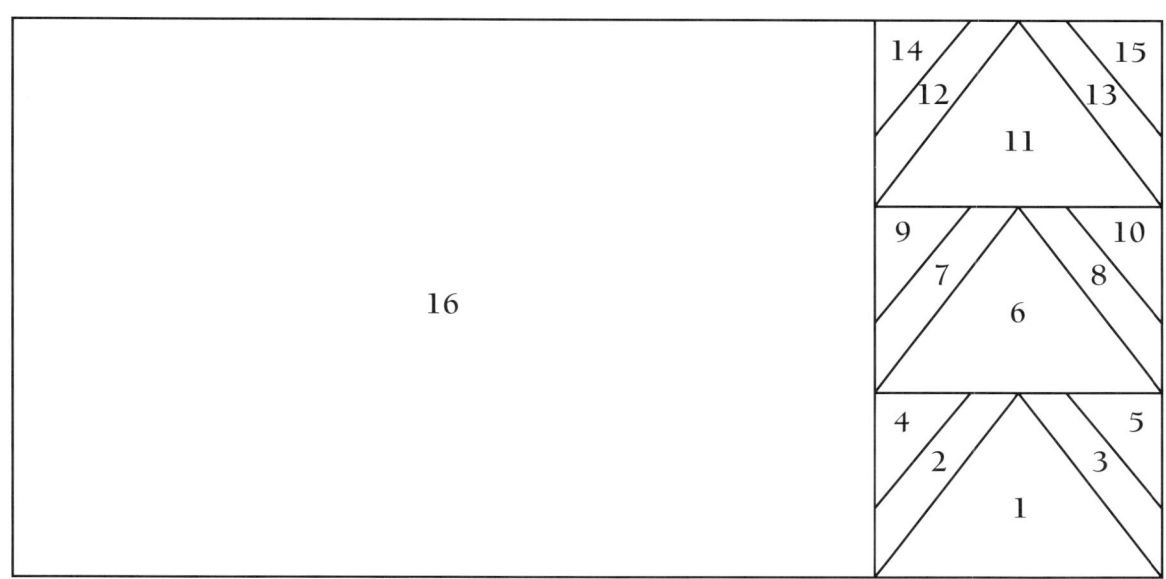

20
Four Square

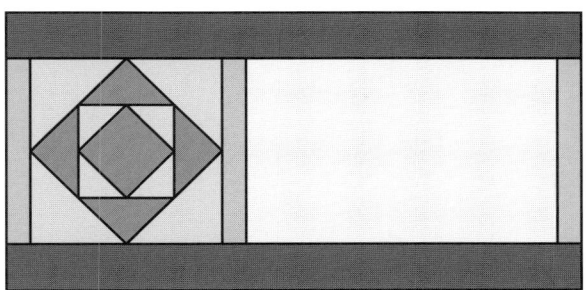

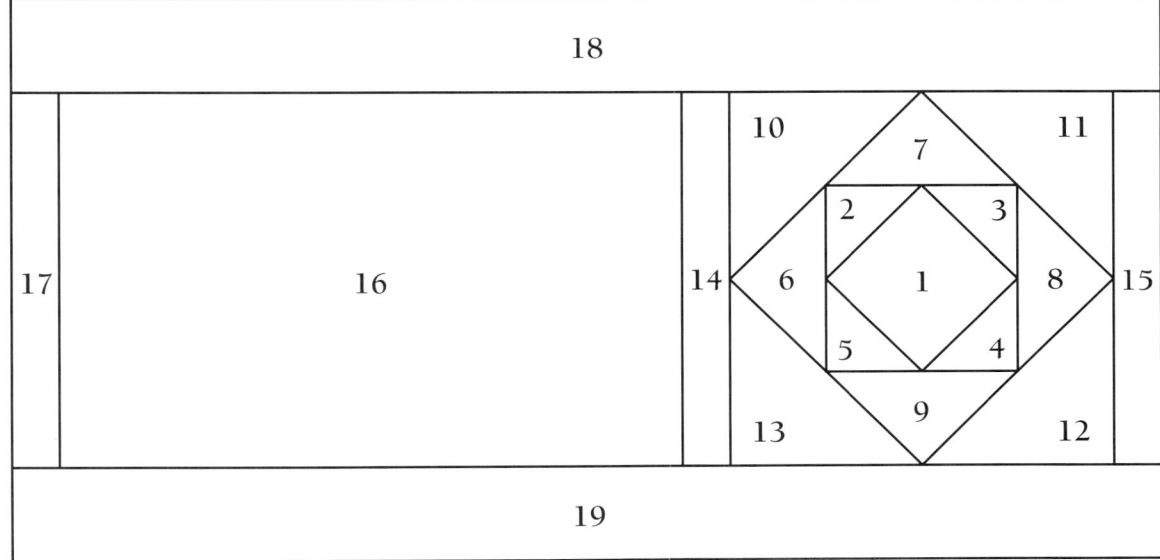

21
Chevrons

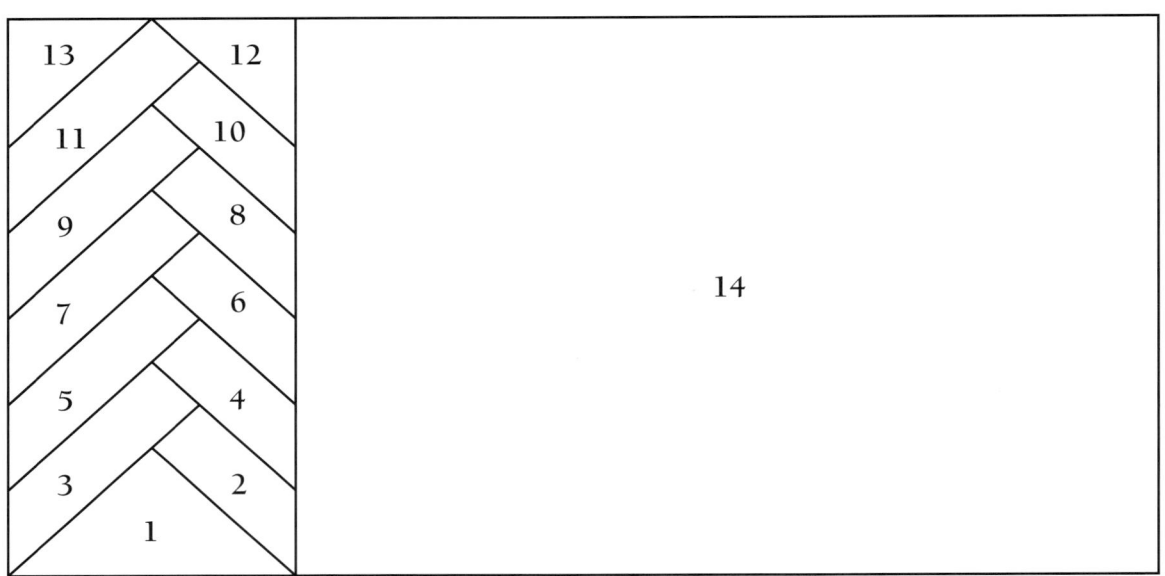

22
Square in a Diamond

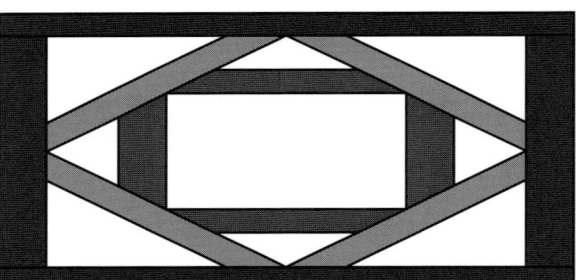

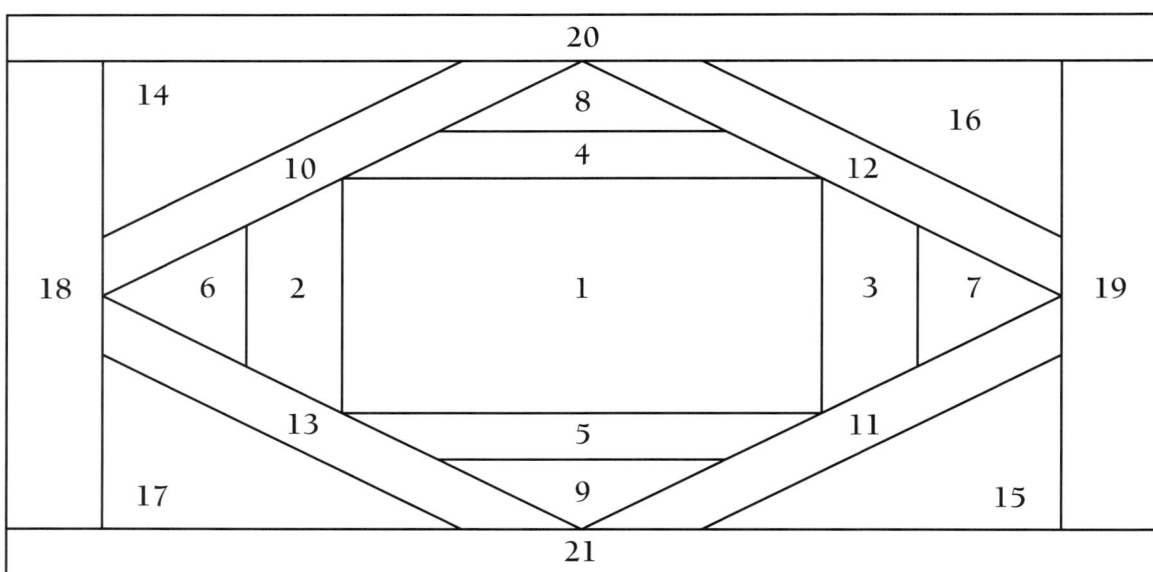

23
Heavenly Angel

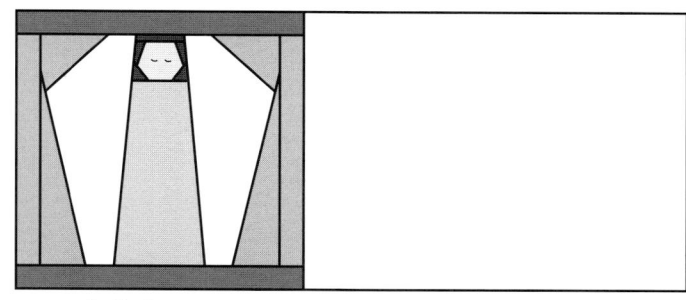

For embellishing, see page 7.

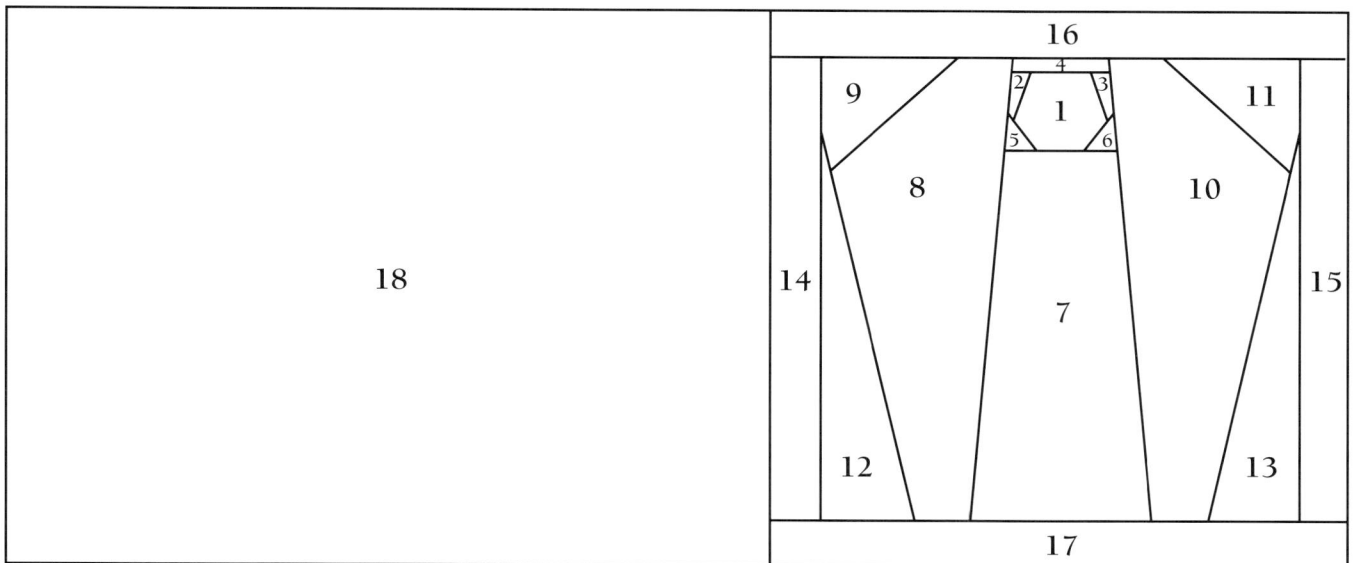

24
Faded Heart

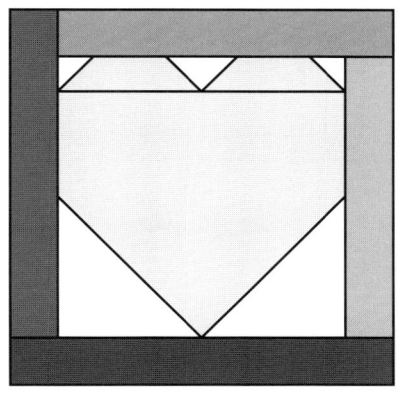
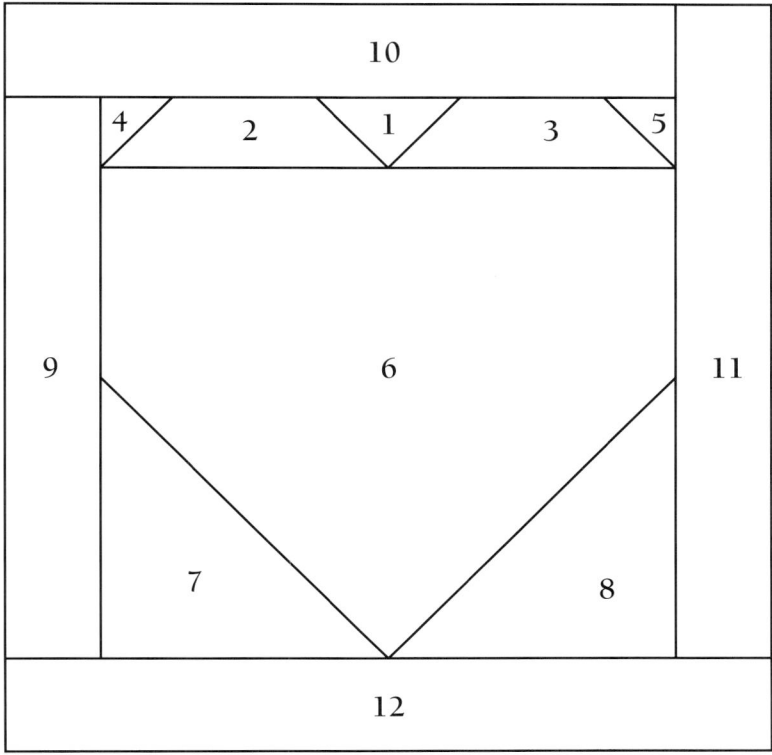

25 Pretty Posy

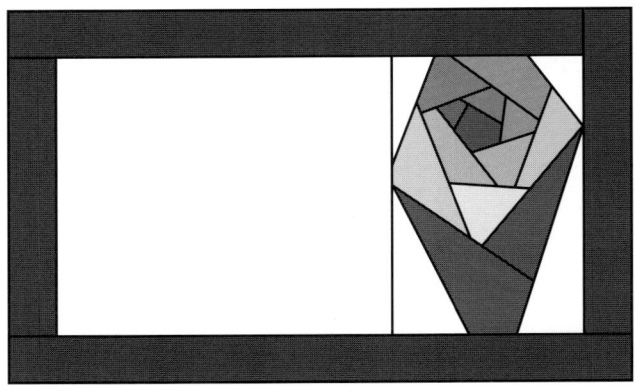

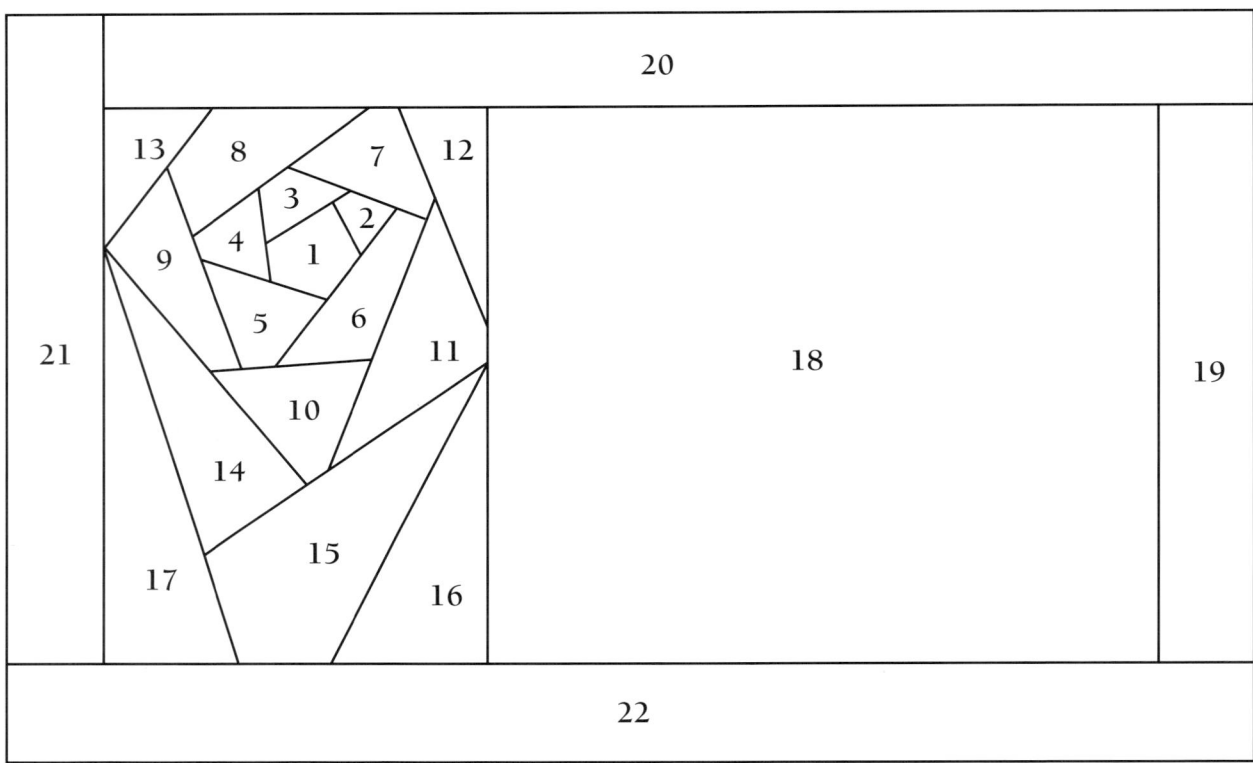

26 Blue Rays

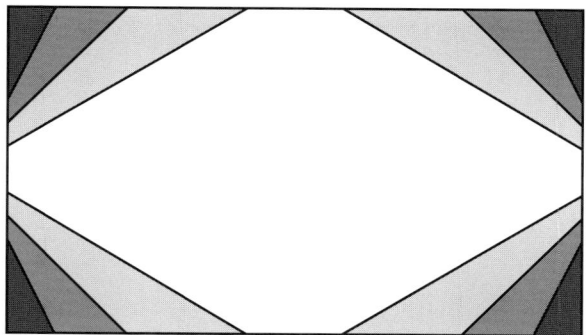

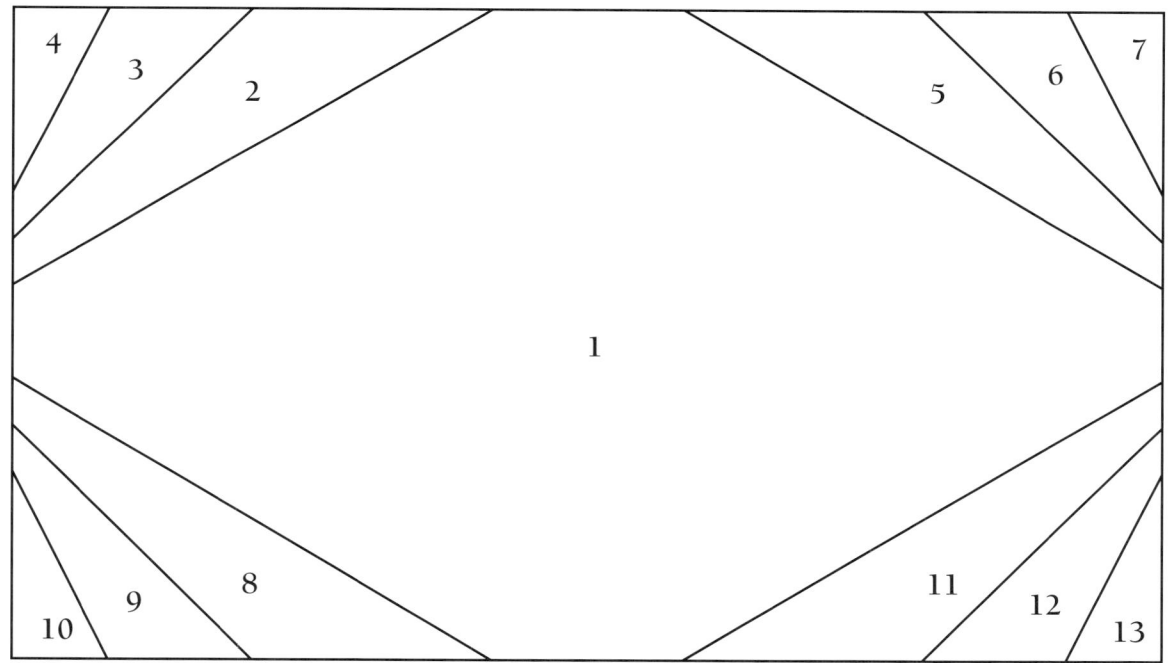

27 Crazy Octagon

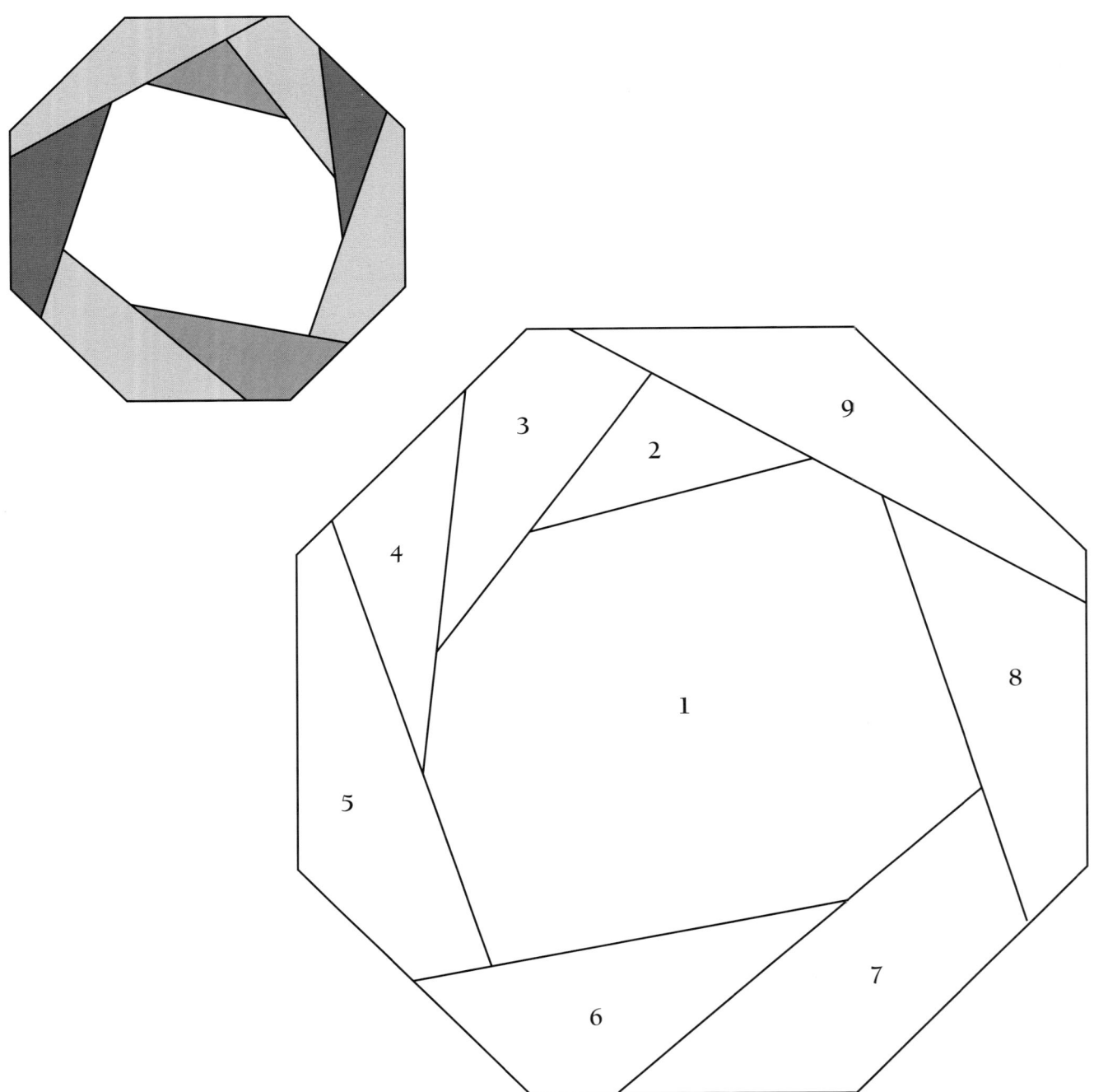

28
Home Sweet Home

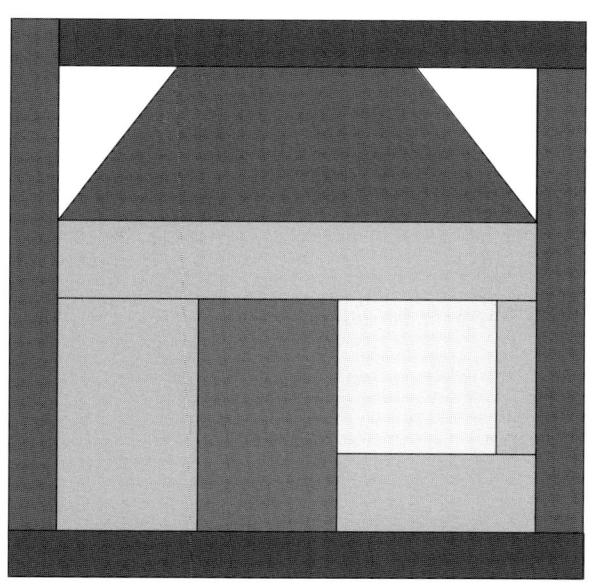

For embellishing, see page 7.

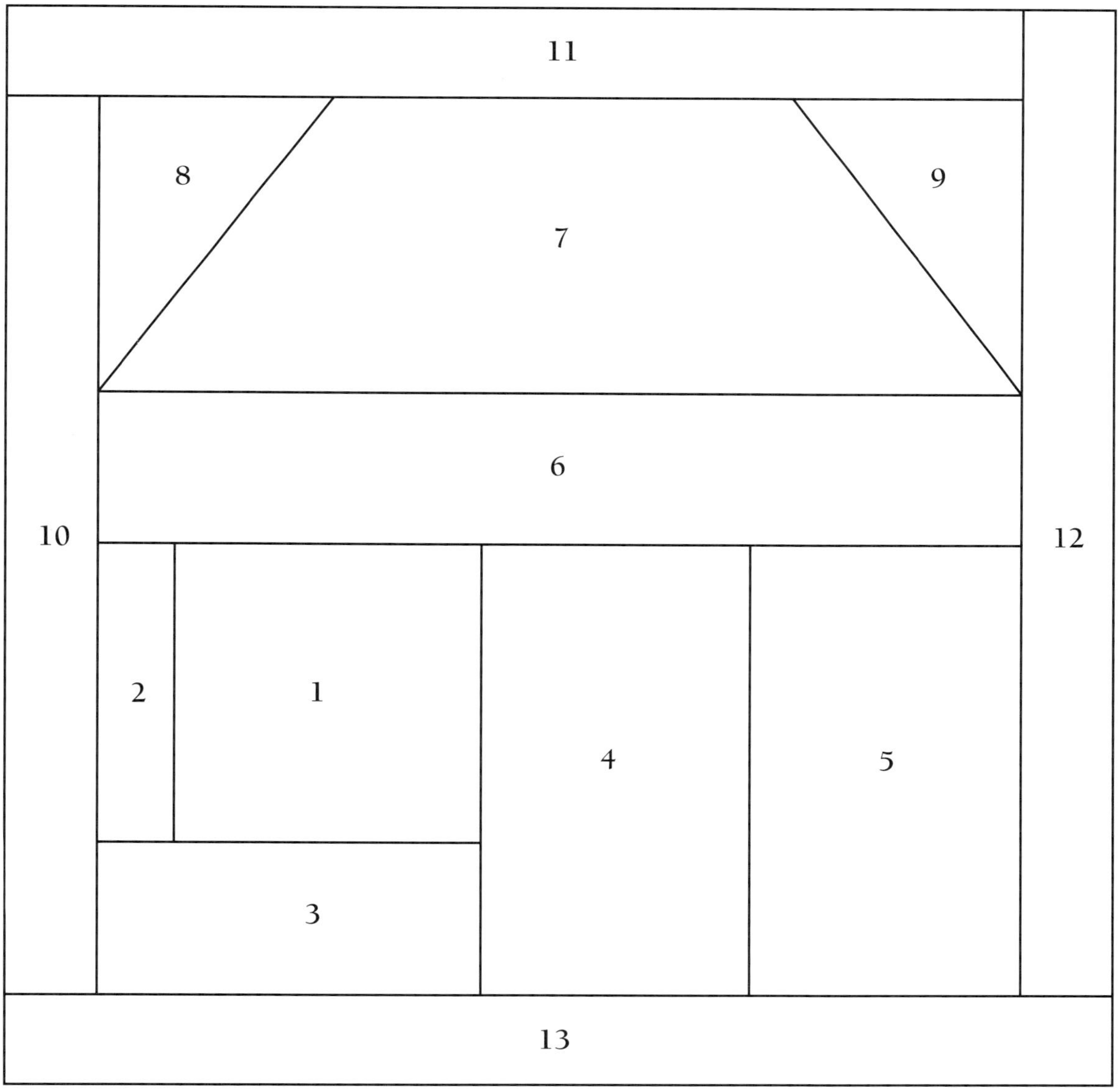

29 Potted Plant

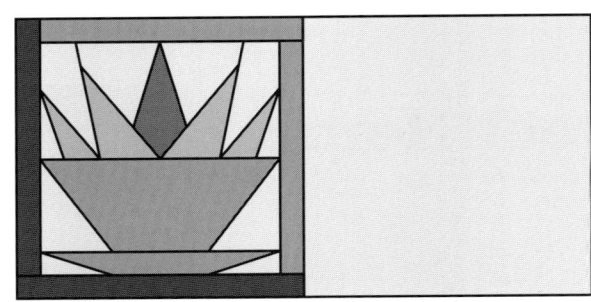

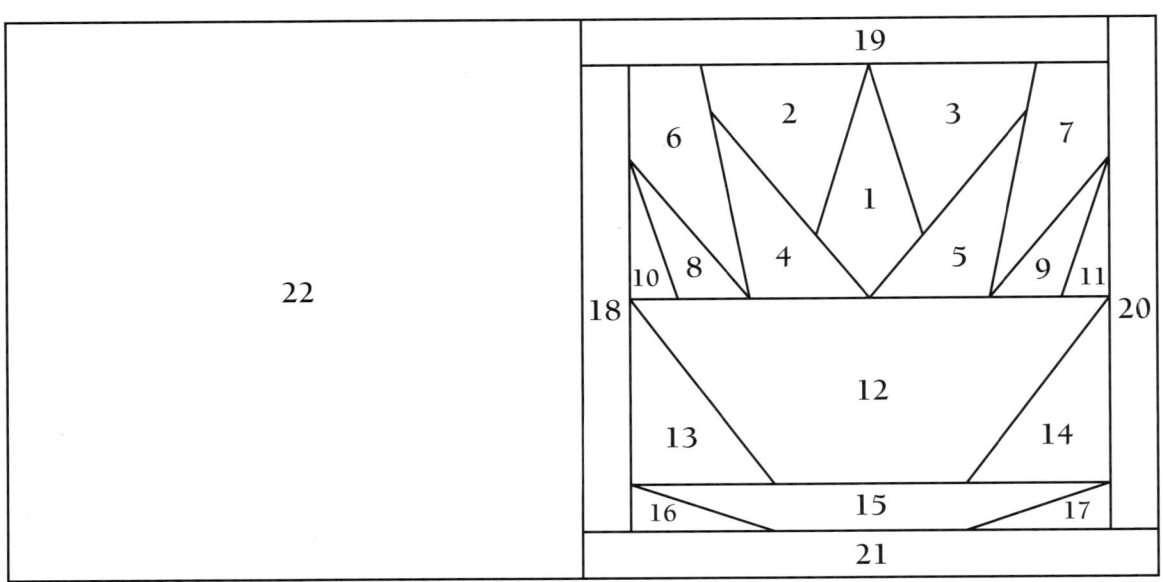

30 Step by Step

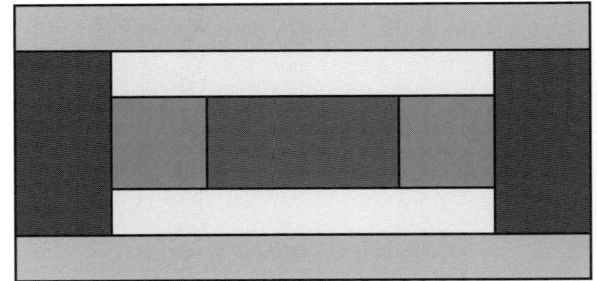